Words for the Journey

Words for the Journey

Ten-Minute Prayer Services for Teachers and Administrators

Lisa Freemantle and Les Miller

NOVALIS

© 2009 Novalis Publishing Inc.

Cover design: Blaine Herrmann
Cover artwork: Lynne McIlvride Evans (www.mcilvride-evans.com)
Layout: Audrey Wells

Published by Novalis
10 Lower Spadina Avenue, Suite 400
Toronto, Ontario, Canada
M5V 2Z2
www.novalis.ca

Library and Archives Canada Cataloguing in Publication

Freemantle, Lisa, 1962-
    Words for the journey : ten-minute prayer services for
teachers and administrators / Lisa Freemantle and Leslie Miller.

ISBN 978-2-89646-142-4

    1. Catholic Church--Liturgy--Texts.
2. Catholic Church--Prayers and devotions.
I. Miller, Leslie, 1952-
II. Title.

BX2170.T43F75 2009   268'.7088282   C2009-903932-X

Printed in Canada.

All rights reserved. No part of this publication may be reproduced, stored in a retrieval system, or transmitted in any form, or by any means, electronic, mechanical, photocopying, recording, or otherwise, without the written permission of the publisher. Purchasers of this book may photocopy individual prayer services to be used by participants at the service.

Unless otherwise noted, the Scripture quotations contained herein are from the New Revised Standard Version of the Bible, copyrighted 1989 by the Division of Christian Education of the National Council of the Churches of Christ in the United States of America, and are used by permission. All rights reserved.

We acknowledge the financial support of the Government of Canada through the Book Publishing Industry Development Program (BPIDP) for our publishing activities.

5 4 3 2 1   13 12 11 10 09

In Gratitude

Thanks to our families for sustaining us while we spent countless hours composing and assembling these prayers. With gratitude, we acknowledge our colleagues at York Catholic District School Board for their support and inspiration, especially those at St. Thomas Aquinas Catholic Elementary School, the Catholic Education Centre, the Faith Ambassadors, and, in particular, Melinda Rapallo, who saw us safely through the first steps on this project, but left the team to prepare for her own journey as a new bride. We are also indebted to the wise and gentle hands of those at Novalis who have safely guided us, particularly Grace Deutsch and Anne Louise Mahoney, as well as consultant Heather Reid. We are most grateful for having the love of God shine on us as we prepared this resource. Our hope is that some light of divine love shines through these words.

Contents

Introduction	9
How to Use This Book	10

September

Our Dreams and Our Cares: Welcoming New Teachers	13
To Be Instruments of Your Healing: A New School Year	14
Jesus the Teacher	16
God Gives Us Courage	18
On Being a Lifelong Learner	19
The Work of Our Hands	20
Encircle Our School (Curriculum Night)	21
Open the Eyes of Our Hearts (Professional Activity Day)	23

October

The Blessed Vocation of Teaching	25
The Season of Autumn	27
A Cloud of Witnesses	28
Gratitude	29
God Has Compassion	30
Discerning Believer	31
True Friends	32
God's Gift of Life	34

November

Lead Us in the Footsteps of the Saints (All Saints' Day)	37
Comfort Us Today (All Souls' Day)	39
Choose Peace (Remembrance Day)	40
A Vision of Justice	42
Building a Civilization of Love (Being a Responsible Citizen)	44
Living Water	46
What Would Jesus Do? (Social Justice)	48
Respect the Word of the Lord	50

December

Healing and Hope (World AIDS Day)	52
Building Bridges Between Parents and Teachers	53
Mary Said "Yes"	54
Advent I: Hope	56
Advent II: Faith	57
Advent III: Joy	58
Advent IV: Love	59
Preparing for Christmas	60

January

New Beginnings (New Year)	62
To Be Your People (Epiphany)	64
The Season of Winter	65
In God's Time	66
We Are United in Christ	68
Being a Collaborative Contributor (Collaboration)	69
The True Nature of God (St. Thomas Aquinas)	71
We Believe	73

February

Sowing the Seeds of Your Love (New Semester)	76
Let Us Celebrate Our Differences	77
Let Us Praise Wisdom	78
God's Love for Us	80
God Will Be There	81
Lead Us into the Desert (Ash Wednesday)	82
Desert, Teach Me (Prayers for Reconciliation)	84
Lent I: Renewal	85

March

Lent II: Sacrifice	88
Lent III: Resisting Temptation	90
Lent IV: To Serve Others	92
Daughters of Faith (International Women's Day)	93
Answer the Call to Persevere	95
March Break Blessing	96
God of the Journey (St. Patrick's Day)	97
You Called Mary (Annunciation)	98

April

Into Jerusalem (Beginning Holy Week)....... 100
Help Us to Love (Stations of the Cross)...... 102
The Upper Room (Holy Thursday) 105
Easter Light 106
Easter Blessing 108
Our Greatest Gift (Reverence) 110
Speak to the Earth (Earth Week)........... 111
Servants of Love
    (Administrative Professionals' Day) 113

May

Model of Love (St. Joseph the Worker) 115
Created in Your Image
    (Catholic Education Week) 116
On Being a Caring Family Member 117
Extraordinary Women (Mother's Day) 119
Let Us Be Responsible.................... 121
The Season of Spring 123
The Fire of the Holy Spirit (Pentecost) 124
Hospitality and Hope
    (The Feast of the Visitation, May 31) 126

June

We Thank You (Retirement) 129
Harmonizing Word and Deed (Integrity)..... 131
Three in One (The Trinity)................ 132
On Being an Effective Communicator 134
Called to Lead.......................... 135
The Season of Summer 137
The Labyrinth of Life 138
Journey into Summer..................... 140

Index 142

Introduction

As members of the Catholic community, we know how important prayer is to our individual and group faith journeys. We pray for many reasons: to worship, to praise, for forgiveness, in thankfulness, in times of rejoicing and in times of sorrow. Prayer allows us to centre ourselves, to relieve stress in the midst of our busy lives where deadlines, report cards, meetings, evaluations and countless other tasks pervade our thoughts. *Words for the Journey* contains 80 original, ready-to-use prayer services that will allow you to pray together on a wide range of themes and occasions.

Purpose

"We are God's servants, working together..."
1 Corinthians 3:9

This compilation of prayer services is designed to help you foster spiritual experiences in your Catholic school community. Catholic education is committed to the ongoing formation of the soul. It is our hope that this resource may help facilitate the communal process of transformation that is central to the mission of our schools. May God bless us as we continue to journey in this mission.

We have each been involved in adult faith formation at the school and board level for many years. As we have found, prayer resources are always in desperate demand, particularly ones that speak to the needs of the educational context. Although we had each compiled a repertoire of prayers for the school setting, we decided that schools would be best served if we were to create new prayer services with them in mind.

An incident that happened to Les during the course of writing this book illustrates the meaning of the title *Words for the Journey*:

I was parked on a downtown street waiting for my family. I used the time to write a prayer for this book. As I was writing, I was disturbed when two young men walked up the street arguing loudly. The smaller of the pair was developmentally challenged. The larger man pushed the smaller man down, swearing at him. I thought to myself, "How can you write a prayer and not act on behalf of a victim?" With that thought, I left the safety of my vehicle and moved to ask about the problem. The aggressor stepped away from his victim and turned his venom on me. Using several single syllable words that are not included in this book, he told me what he thought of my intervention. The victim fled and the aggressor stalked off.

Our tradition tells us that prayers need to be completed through action. Prayer nurtures the heart, brings us closer to God and helps to break down barriers that separate us. But God wants us to heal this wounded world as well. Prayer can give us words for our journey to help build the "Civilization of Love" (a term used by Pope Paul VI at a papal audience on December 31, 1975, and repeated often by Pope John Paul II). The prayers in this resource can sustain us as we journey to many different places as educators.

We believe that within these pages you will find prayer services that will nourish your spirits, open your hearts and accompany you as you travel along your individual faith journeys. May you rejoice, thank, worship and praise our God as you pray these *Words for the Journey*.

Lisa and Les

How to Use This Book

The prayer services in *Words for the Journey* can be used as introductions to staff meetings, at the beginning or closing events on Professional Activity Days, during informal staff gatherings, or as stand-alone times of prayer. The topics, which are organized by month, were selected according to both liturgical and secular themes. Each prayer service should begin and end with the sign of the cross. Where it is not written explicitly in the text, we indicate this with a "+".

Preparing Well for a Prayer Service

- *Assess the needs of the community*

Prayer time should be a positive experience for all. The primary aim of a faith development program is to enlighten and support staff members and to offer spiritual growth through faith-forming prayers and reflections. When planning opportunities for formation, begin by assessing the needs and interests of the school community. This will help you determine the spiritual health of the community and provide a starting point.

As you plan each liturgy, remember that people have different

- life experiences,
- ways of praying,
- degrees of spiritual awareness,
- ways of relating to others, and
- comfort levels with self-disclosure.

Move forward gently. As participants become more familiar with the group and format, facilitators can eventually provide more

- sharing of personal reflections and prayers,
- time for silence, and
- time for prayer.

- *Create a sacred space*

What makes the Catholic school distinctive is its attempt to generate a community climate in the school that is permeated by the Gospel spirit of freedom and love.

—Pope Paul VI,
Declaration on Christian Education, #8

A visual focal point is appropriate for a liturgical gathering. Each prayer service in this resource contains suggestions for how to prepare the space, including rituals and table dressing ideas, that can enrich your prayer experiences. The approach can be as simple as a tablecloth, a Bible, and a candle. You can also add icons and sacred symbols such as a cross as you create sacred space.

- *Choose readers ahead of time*

Choose readers and give them a copy of the liturgy ahead of time so they can prepare before the service.

- *Aim for the participation of all*

Prayer time should allow for the full, conscious and active participation of all. This can be achieved through spontaneous prayer and through communal prayer and responses. Scripture reflections in this book are intended to be read aloud. Each participant, therefore, will need a copy of the service.

Make sure that all can follow along: before prayer begins, explain any logistical elements, such as instructions for a ritual.

- *Explore options for the service*

Feel free to make the services your own and to vary your approach from one service to the next. Here are a few suggestions:

- before you begin, invite participants to name aloud those for whom they wish to pray;
- incorporate music;
- include the doxology (*For the kingdom, the power and the glory are yours, now and forever*) at the end of the Lord's Prayer;
- include the Alleluia before Gospel readings (if the Alleluia is not sung, it is omitted).

- *Review the experience*

Ask for informal feedback to learn about the group's prayer experience. Make notes and keep their comments in mind for future prayer celebrations. Invite participants to share how the group prayer is helping them in their life and work. Spiritual growth is a continuous process that requires reflection.

May your prayer services bring you peace, clarity and joy, and may God speak to your heart as you pray these *Words for the Journey*.

September

Our Dreams and Our Cares: Welcoming New Teachers

[Rely] on the power of God, who saved us and called us with a holy calling.
(2 Timothy 1:8)

Preparation: *Create a focal point for prayer using some of the following elements: candle, Bible, flowers and symbols of the community (such as an image of the school's patron). Select readers.*

Opening Prayer

+God of love,
Jesus the teacher,
Spirit of wisdom,
we place our dreams and our cares before you.
Be with us in our hope and in our anxiety;
in our learning and in our friendships.
Let us know that you are always
walking with us,
giving us courage and strength
for the journey through the school year.
Amen.

Ritual

Leader: Let us welcome one another
with a sign of greeting and peace.

All exchange a sign of peace.

Scripture: Matthew 4:18-22

Scripture Reflection

Dear Jesus,
help us to see ourselves as disciples.
Transform our work into vocation.
May we drop our nets of fear, distraction
and misunderstanding.
Let us follow you along the shores of our lives,
through the mountains and valleys,
even though our paths lead to Calvary,
because Calvary leads to the empty tomb.
Bless our calling.

Litany: For the Way Ahead

Loving God,
When we tire,
All: Watch over us.
When we become dry,
All: Enliven us.
When we despair,
All: Give us hope.
When we grow,
All: Strengthen us.
When we create,
All: Inspire us.
May we always be aware that you are
walking with us at school and at home.
Bless our vocation as educators,
you who know what it means to teach
the willing and the worried,
the eager and the wounded,
the grateful and the greedy.
Hold us close in our daily work.
Touch the hearts of students and help us
to build a Civilization of Love.
Amen.

Closing Prayer

God of love,
bless the new teachers gathered here today
with faith, hope and love.
Guide their days.
Bless them with health and strength.
Bless them with joy for the journey.
We make this prayer in the name of Jesus
the teacher.
+**Amen.**

To Be Instruments of Your Healing: A New School Year

This month shall mark for you the beginning of months.
(Exodus 12:2)

Preparation: *Fill a bowl with water. (If possible, use holy water.) You may wish to have music playing during the water ritual. Select readers.*

Opening Prayer

+Loving God,
you call us to be disciples:
to be instruments of your **healing**,
reaching out to your beloved **children**;
to be instruments of your **hope**,
helping to make learning **more effective**;
to be instruments of your **harmony**, bringing
understanding where there is confusion.
Gracious God, flow through **us**
in the year ahead
and help us bring peace
to our beautiful yet broken **world**.
Amen.

Ritual

Leader: Our baptism was **a new** beginning for us in the family of God. Let us remember today that we live out our **baptism** by helping to establish God's reign in our world, by making our school open **to** the flow of the Holy Spirit.

All dip their hands into the bowl of water as a reminder of their baptism and Christian commitment.

Scripture: Mark 1:9-11

Scripture Reflection

God of love,
may our baptism remind us
that we are made for loving.
Help us to live out our baptismal promises
in your service.
Help us this year to make our school
a place where your love reigns.
Bless the students in this school.
May those who are new to the school
feel welcomed.
May those who will be graduating
extend their gifts of leadership.
And may the staff of this school grow in
their love for you and for this community.
Amen.

Litany: For the New School Year

Creator God,
you have blessed us
with goodness and love.
May our work this year be a worthy echo
of your grace,
may our reflections be guided
by your wisdom, and
may our celebrations be touched by your joy.
During this school year,
let us continue to grow in love for you
and in respect for one another.
Let us learn to see with your eyes.
Help us to see you
All: In stranger and friend;
To see you
All: In young and old;

To see you
All: In the happy and the sad;
To see you
All: In the hurt and the healing;
To see you
All: In success and struggle;
To see you
All: In the popular and the unpopular;
To see you
All: In the wise and the foolish;
To see you
All: In male and female;
To see you
All: In listening and speaking;
To see you
All: In hearts and minds;
To see you
All: In all of us, all the time, everywhere.

May this vision
bring joy into our hearts when we are sad,
calm into our souls
when we are troubled, and
justice into our actions
when we see wrongdoing.
Amen.

Closing Prayer

Spirit of wisdom,
help us to remember
that we are **made** in God's image
and that we **have the responsibility**
to cherish **our lives** as God's gift to each of us.
Gracious God,
you have **gifted to** us the gift of our humanity.
May we use **our gifts** to create schools
where love **and** justice reign
and where **wisdom** and responsibility
can be seen in **our** actions.
+**Amen.**

Jesus the Teacher

*Jesus went throughout Galilee,
teaching in their synagogues
and proclaiming the good news of the kingdom.*
(Matthew 4:23)

Preparation: *On the prayer table, place a lit candle. Surround the candle with school supplies (such as pencils, erasers, rulers, paper) and a Bible. Select readers.*

Introduction

From a very young age, Jesus spent a lot of time teaching. He taught the ways of God in the synagogues, in the streets, in people's homes, and in the wilderness. He taught learned rabbis and Pharisees. He taught the poor, the wealthy, the lonely and the outcast. His students included young and old, men and women. His message was one of love, faith, healing, joy and peace. He spoke of forgiveness and vengeance, of light and darkness, of sin and forgiveness, of despair and hope. He wanted the world to know about the glory of God's kingdom.

Let us begin with a prayer of praise to Jesus our teacher. We begin our prayer with the sign of the cross.

Litany: Jesus Our Teacher

Jesus, we look to you for leadership, guidance and example.
All: Jesus, you are our leader.
You lead us in the way to God and we follow.
All: Jesus, you are our guidance.
You guide us in the way of truth and light, and we follow.
All: Jesus, you are our example.
We look at your life's example, at your ways, and we follow.
All: Jesus, you are our leader, our guidance, our example;
Jesus, you are our teacher.
**All: Lead us to God.
Guide us in your goodness.
Teach us to follow your example.**

Scripture: Mark 1:21-28

Reflection

This teacher didn't use lesson plans or follow a curriculum. He didn't file long-range plans. He didn't mark or assign grades to work submitted to him. He didn't write report cards or conduct parent-teacher interviews. His classroom had no books or pencils or desks. His school had no walls or specified hours of operation. He did not have a teaching degree from university. There were no age limits or special documents required to get into his classes. There were no late slips or detentions in his school. He had no teacher's pets and played no favourites. Yet his lessons have moved generations of believers. His teachings are studied by scholars around the world. His words have been internalized, memorized, written down and shared over and over again by the millions of students who have loved him and followed him faithfully for over 20 centuries.

Who is this amazing teacher?
Jesus, the greatest teacher of all.

Responsorial Prayer

Leader: We pray to Jesus, our rabbi, our teacher. May our prayers reflect the love we have for one another and for our Saviour. The response is:
Rabbi Jesus, hear our prayer.

Jesus, your lessons are the way of truth.
May we study the parables you told
and learn from them
how best to serve God
as we strive to reach the kingdom.
We pray to our Teacher. **R.**

Jesus, you spoke to us
about loving our enemies.
May we learn how to forgive
those who wrong us
and turn our enemies into our friends.
We pray to our Teacher. **R.**

Jesus, your message to us was one of charity for the poor, hope for the marginalized, and love for the friendless.
May we learn to put into practice
all you have taught about justice,
and always try to remember
what you would do.
We pray to our Teacher. **R.**

Jesus, you taught us that there are times
to celebrate and indulge
with friends and family,
and times to abstain from these
in quiet prayer.
May we know when to feast
and when to fast.
We pray to our Teacher. **R.**

May the prayers we make today
infuse our souls with an even greater sense
of your teachings.
We ask this through Christ,
our Lord and our Teacher. **Amen.**

Let us pray to God in the words that Jesus taught us:
Our Father ...

Closing Prayer

Loving God, we thank you for Jesus, our beloved teacher. May we strive to be teachers like him who see the whole student and not just the marks on the paper before us. We make this prayer in the name of Jesus.
+**Amen.**

God Gives Us Courage

Do not be afraid.
(Luke 1:30)

Preparation: *Place a lit pillar candle on the prayer table. Divide participants into two groups, A and B. Select a reader.*

Invitation to Prayer

Courage is the moral fortitude to do what is right. It does not necessarily denote bravery, which implies heroism and lack of fear in the face of danger. Rather, courage is the will to do the right thing no matter what the personal consequences. There is no such thing as courage without fear. Jesus is our model of courage. Let us now open our hearts to his guidance in our prayers today.

+Scripture: Luke 21:9-19

Litany: God Gives Us Courage

Group A: God gives us courage
to face the unknowns of everyday life.
Group B: We know that whatever
the day holds,
God will help us tackle any situation.
We are never alone.
God will be there.
Group A: God gives us courage
to face evil and resist temptation.
Group B: We know that whatever evils beset us,
God will gently guide us on the right path.
God will be there.
Group A: God gives us courage
to deal with our failings.
Group B: We know that despite our sins,
God will always love us.
God will be there.
Group A: God gives us courage
to stop the fighting in our world.
Group B: We know that peace
begins with us.
God will be there.
Group A: God gives us courage
to explore new challenges.
Group B: We know that God never gives us more than we can handle.
God will be there.
Group A: God gives us courage
to face the eventual end of our lives.
Group B: We know that death is only a step in the journey to his kingdom.
God will be there.
Group A: God gives us courage.
With God's help, we can calm oceans of fury,
move mountains of ambivalence,
soothe forests of fear,
change winds of hatred.
Group B: We know that with God
we can bring about caring, peace,
serenity and love.
God gives us the courage to do these
and more.
**All: God will always be there.
God gives us courage.
Amen.**

Closing Prayer

God our strength,
with you on our side, we can do anything.
With you at our side, we can go anywhere.
With you in our midst, we can be free.
Thank you, God, for giving us the courage
to deal with the unknowns in life.
+Amen.

On Being a Lifelong Learner

Give me understanding...
(Psalm 119:125)

Preparation: *Arrange the prayer space with symbols of learning, such as a lamp, yearbook, Bible, scroll, mortarboard. Select readers.*

Opening Prayer

+God of wisdom,
you call us to grow in your grace
with hearts to love you,
with souls open to you,
with minds to learn from you.
Help us to see beyond distractions
and keep our vision clear –
a vision of your reign.
Amen.

Scripture: Mark 10:17-25

Scripture Reflection

Brother Jesus,
with deep wisdom,
you taught the wealthy young man.
May we listen to our young with compassion,
as you listened to others.
May we instruct learners
to create deeper understanding,
as you taught your followers.
May we lovingly challenge students
to move them to deeper truth,
as you challenge us.
You are the master Teacher.
Let us know that you are walking
with us always.

Litany: For the Learner

Loving God,
you challenge us to be learners
throughout our lives.
Amid gifts and grumbles,
All: Let us learn from you.
When journeying and resting,
All: Let us learn from you.
When hurting and healing,
All: Let us learn from you.
In wonder and wandering,
All: Let us learn from you.
In action and reflection,
All: Let us learn from you.
In sanctuary and danger,
All: Let us learn from you.

Lead us, loving God,
towards wisdom and love,
along peaceful paths, hand in hand.
Lead us. Inspire us. Challenge us.
Amen.

Closing Prayer

Loving God,
our creator, our friend, our companion,
bless our journey of learning.
Refresh our souls and renew our spirits.
Lead us in paths of wisdom,
compassion and understanding.
Bless us with an enduring love of learning.
May the Holy Spirit flow freely
through the classrooms and halls
of our school,
through the rooms and gardens of our home,
through our churches and workplaces.
We make this prayer in the name of Jesus.
+**Amen.**

The Work of Our Hands

*Let the favour of the Lord our God be upon us,
and prosper for us the work of our hands.*
(Psalm 90:17)

Preparation: *At the focal point of prayer, place symbols of the different work roles in your school (for example, a planning document to represent a teacher, a file folder for a secretary, a mop for a custodian). Designate a representative for each form of work. Select readers.*

Opening Prayer

+Loving God,
you call us to be your disciples,
to work by your side as
instruments of your healing,
reaching out to your beloved children;
instruments of your hope,
helping to make learning more effective;
instruments of your harmony,
bringing understanding
where there is confusion.
Gracious God,
continue to flow through us,
that we may continue to bring peace
to our beautiful yet broken world.
Amen.

Scripture: Matthew 6:25-34

Scripture Reflection

Whatever we do, O Lord,
let it be done for your sake.
As long as we work,
let it be done for you,
As long as we plan,
let it be done in your name.
As long as we strive,
let it be guided by you.

Each representative of a role comes forward, raises the appropriate symbol, and names the role. All respond: **We give thanks**.

Litany: To the Spirit of Virtue

Spirit of courage,
All: Lead us from fear.
Spirit of compassion,
All: Lead us from selfishness.
Spirit of justice,
All: Lead us from persecution.
Spirit of hope,
All: Lead us from despair.
Spirit of unity,
All: Lead us from isolation.
Spirit of wisdom,
All: Lead us from ignorance.
Holy Spirit,
guide our schools and our world
to a more peaceful and just existence.
Amen.

Closing Prayer

Loving God,
Bless our work.
May it help build your reign.
May it lead to the healing
of our broken world.
May it touch hearts and comfort wounds.
May it create sacred places where your love
shines through.
May all we do be done for you.
+Amen.

Encircle Our School (Curriculum Night)

*One thing I asked of the Lord,
that will I seek after:
to live in the house of the Lord
all the days of my life.*
(Psalm 27:4)

Preparation: *Arrange the chairs in a circle. For the parts marked Reader 1 and Reader 2, select two readers or assign the parts to two halves of the circle (e.g., left side is Reader 1 and right side is Reader 2).*

Opening Prayer

+God of love,
we are seated in a circle today
to symbolize your love
that encircles this community.
Let us now reflect as a community
on the school environment
we would like to create and nurture
for ourselves and our students.

Loving God,
encircle this school
and keep these good things within:
eagerness to learn,
the flowering of talents,
a sense of wonder,
enjoyment of sport,
experiences of beauty,
the warmth of friendship,
the art of listening,
respect for all,
service to others,
teamwork between young people and adults,
care for the planet,
reverence for life, and
balance of body, mind and spirit.

Loving God,
encircle this school
and keep these harmful things outside:
low self-esteem,
confusion,
prejudice,
arrogance,
bullying,
cheating,
stealing,
malicious gossip,
apathy, and
cynicism.

Loving God,
encircle this school,
for you are the source
of all that is good and true.
We ask for this blessing in your name.
Amen.

Scripture Reflection
(adapted from 1 Corinthians 13:1-13)

Reader 1: Our years in Catholic schools
have helped us know
how to love ourselves,
our friends,
our God.
Reader 2: Let us read and reflect on
this adaptation of St. Paul's great hymn
to Love,
found in his first letter to the Corinthians.
Reader 1: If I may speak words well enough
to sway a meeting,
but do not have love,
I have become a noisy gong
or a clanging cymbal.

Reader 2: If I have the gift of prophecy,
and can speak out for justice,
and if I have all faith,
so as to remove mountains,
but do not have love,
I am nothing.
Reader 1: And if I give all my money
to feed the poor,
and if I work until midnight,
but do not have love,
I have gained nothing.
Reader 2: Love is patient
Reader 1: With students, parents
and colleagues.
Reader 2: Love is kind and not jealous,
Reader 1: But rejoices in each other's
successes.
Reader 2: Love is not arrogant,
Reader 1: But shares the joys of handing
down wisdom to the next generation.
Reader 2: Love is not rude,
Reader 1: But treats adversaries with respect
and dignity.
Reader 2: Love does not bear grudges,
Reader 1: But practises reconciliation.
Reader 2: Love does not enjoy other's pain,
Reader 1: But is at home with peace.
Reader 2: Love bears all things,
Reader 1: Even impossible deadlines.
Reader 2: Love believes all things
Reader 1: Coming from God.
Reader 2: Love hopes all things,
Reader 1: That harmony and peace
will prevail.
Reader 2: Love never fails,
Reader 1: Despite shattered dreams.
Reader 2: When we were young,
we used to speak like children,
think like children,
reason like children.

Reader 1: Now that we are leaders of children,
we leave behind childish ways of thinking.
Reader 2: Even now I can only just begin
to understand the love of God.
Reader 1: But later,
when we are face to face with God,
we will know fully.
Reader 2: But for now,
faith, hope and love reign in our hearts,
Readers 1 & 2: But the greatest of these
is love.
Reader 1: May God bless all those
who are part of circles of loving:
our families and friends,
our students and colleagues,
and the whole People of God.
Reader 2: May we continue to live out
these blessings in the years to come,
always aware that Jesus is walking with us.
Amen.

Closing Prayer

God of hope,
may we follow the guidance of Jesus
in coming to the rescue of those
who are imprisoned.
May those who are in prison for the wrong
they have done
feel your loving presence.
May those who are in prisons of fear
of being bullied or harassed by others
feel your loving presence.
May those who are in prisons of physical
or emotional suffering
feel your loving presence.
May those who cannot or will not hear
your message of love
feel your loving presence.
We make this prayer
through Jesus the teacher of love.
+**Amen.**

Open the Eyes of Our Hearts (Professional Activity Day)

Keep your heart with all vigilance.
(Proverbs 4:23)

Preparation: *Create a focal point for prayer with a Bible, cross and a candle. Select readers.*

Opening Prayer

+God of creation,
open the eyes of our hearts
to a sense of beauty
amid the greyness of routine.
Splash colours of surprise
in the desert of apathy.
Bless us with an oasis of care amid
the landscape of problems and worries.
Send angels of proportion and balance.
Send angels of sense and truth
to heal us so that we may heal others.
May our learning draw us closer to you.
May we be revitalized in our commitment
to your work in this school.
May we be blessings of hope and gratitude
to our world.
Amen.

Ritual

Leader: Let us now share a sign of peace with each other.

All exchange a sign of peace.

Scripture: Ephesians 1:15-19

Reflection

Today, we hear St. Paul affirm the Christian community in Ephesus. Like this fledgling community, we are asked to look with the eyes of the heart at the challenges we face at our school; to see them not just as problems to be solved but as mysteries to be embraced. We are also asked to view the items on our agenda from a higher perspective, through eyes of justice, love and hope. We know that God is presiding over our gathering today.

Litany: For Vision

All: Open the eyes of our hearts
When sadness obscures joy.
All: Open the eyes of our hearts
When selfishness clouds compassion.
All: Open the eyes of our hearts
When greed blinds generosity.
All: Open the eyes of our hearts
When resentment obliterates gratitude.
All: Open the eyes of our hearts
When fear darkens love.
All: Open the eyes of our hearts
To our families.
All: Open the eyes of our hearts
To our students.
All: Open the eyes of our hearts
To our colleagues.
All: Open the eyes of our hearts
To those in our community.
All: Open the eyes of our hearts
To those in our country.
All: Open the eyes of our hearts
To all people on this planet.

Closing Prayer

God of gatherings,
bless us and walk with us today.
We make this prayer in the name of Jesus.
+Amen.

October

The Blessed Vocation of Teaching

Take heart; get up, he is calling you.
(Mark 10:49)

Preparation: *Symbols of teaching may be used for the focal point of the service. Select readers, including nine for the Closing Prayer. "The Teacher Came to Our School" is intended to be read dramatically by a single reader.*

Opening Prayer

+Loving God,
bless our hearts,
bless our souls,
bless this gathering.
We thank you for this grace-filled world.
Give us strength and wisdom
to proclaim your goodness and love
to the young.
May our minds be open to the subtle ways
you flow through our lives.
This we pray in the name of Jesus.
Amen.

The Teacher Came to Our School

The news arrived:
the Teacher was coming to our school.
We all had our say:
he will teach Industrial Arts,
for he was a carpenter;
he will teach English,
for he taught in parables;
he will teach Special Education,
for he was always on the side of the underdog;
he will teach Science and Math,
for he is the Master of the laws of nature;
he will teach Arts,
for he is the Lord of the Dance;
he will teach Family Studies,
for he is the host of the heavenly banquet;
he will teach Modern Languages,
for he understands every tongue;
he will teach Business,
for his justice is sorely needed;
he will teach Phys. Ed.,
for he has unbounded strength;
he will teach Geography and History,
for he has travelled every land
and lived for all of time;
he will teach Law,
for he confounded the Scribes
and the Pharisees;
he will teach Guidance,
for he is the Light of the World;
he will be a secretary,
for he knows all our words;
he will be a custodian,
because he came to serve;
he will be an administrator,
for he is the master Teacher.
At last, the Dean of Religion said knowingly,
"He undoubtedly will be in our department,
for what greater vocation can there be
than to teach love?"
But on the day the Teacher came,
he came to sit in a chair facing the board,
late, chewing gum and out of uniform.

Scripture: John 13:12-17

Reflection

All: My profession is a noble one.
I am a teacher.
My profession is a noble one.
I am a teacher.

Reader 1: I walk in the footsteps
of Socrates, Plato and Aristotle;
All: I know that the unexamined life is not worth living.

Reader 2: I walk in the footsteps
of Confucius, Lao Tze and Buddha;
All: I know that wisdom is found in truth and balance.

Reader 3: I walk in the footsteps
of Isaiah, Ezekiel and Jeremiah;
All: I know that those who speak to God will suffer rejection.

Reader 4: I walk in the footsteps
of Jesus of Nazareth;
All: I know that my words and deeds must speak of the kingdom of love.

Reader 5: I walk in the footsteps
of St. Paul, St. Robert Bellarmine,
St. Augustine and St. Thomas Aquinas;
All: I know that learning can make the world holy.

Reader 6: I walk in the footsteps
of St. Francis, St. Teresa and St. Ignatius;
All: I know that we are the arms and hands of Christ that do his work.

Reader 7: I walk in the footsteps
of Anne Sullivan and Helen Keller;
All: I know that God has graced me with weaknesses
so that I may know my strengths.

Reader 8: I walk in the footsteps
of Martin Buber and Victor Frankl;
All: I know that God consecrates the desk to become an altar.

Reader 9: I walk in the footsteps
of Dorothy Day, Jean Vanier
and Mother Teresa;
All: I know that the heart of learning is the heart of the teacher.

All: My profession is a noble one.
I am a teacher.
My profession is a noble one.
I am a teacher.

Closing Prayer

Loving God,
bless the teachers here
with courage and commitment,
passion and patience,
integrity and inspiration.
May we be living examples
of your Good News.
We make this prayer
in the name of Jesus the teacher.
+Amen.

The Season of Autumn

[There is] a time to pluck up what is planted.
(Ecclesiastes 3:2)

Preparation: *Place a red tablecloth on the prayer centre. Place on it a large plate of coloured leaves. In the centre of the plate, light a red pillar candle. Divide participants into two groups. Have representatives from each group add ripe fruit, brightly coloured gourds and corn to the table during the Litany. Select readers.*

Opening Prayer

+God of the seasons,
you paint the world in a glorious array
during the autumn.
We wake up to a world
filled with colour and plenty.
The mighty trees show off their splendour.
The harvests show us the ripened fruit
of our labours.
We praise you for this wonderful season.
Help us to appreciate all the wonder
of our world.
We ask this through your Son, Jesus Christ.
Amen.

Scripture: Joel 2:23-24

Litany: Autumn

Group 1: To the north, to the east
to the south, to the west,
Leader: No matter where we look during the season of autumn, we see that God shows us the wonders of our world, the glory of creation, the splendours of life.
Group 2: Inward, outward and all around us,
Leader: At every turn and within our hearts, we feel God's great love for us.
With every breath we take,
and with every glance around us,
we know that God is always with us.
**All: For God graces us children
with the season of autumn.**

Leader: God blesses us with rainbows
of rich colours,
Group 1: Painted forests
and feathered heather,
Group 2: Fresh, crisp mornings,
brisk and cool,
Group 1: Rich shades of ochre, plum,
maroon and deep red,
Group 2: Bountiful harvests of fruit
and of wheat.

Group 1: From the north, from the east,
from the south, from the west,
Leader: No matter where we look,
and at every turn,
**All: God graces us children
with the season of autumn.**

Closing Prayer

God of the seasons,
We praise you in thanksgiving
for the season of autumn.
Your paintbrush fills the world
with glorious colour.
By the grace of your will, we are blessed
with bountiful harvests.
May we, your children, celebrate
the earth's beauty
and be ever thankful for the plentiful riches
you bestow on us.
+Amen.

A Cloud of Witnesses

Since we are surrounded by so great a cloud of witnesses, let us also lay aside every weight and the sin that clings so closely, and let us run with perseverance the race that is set before us.
(Hebrews 12:1)

Preparation: *Create a prayer focal point using icons or images from the Internet of the people mentioned in this service. Select readers.*

Opening Prayer

+God of justice,
you have blessed us with memory and vision:
memory to walk with the clouds of
witnesses to goodness and righteousness,
and vision to see hope and compassion
sweeping through our world.
Guide our searching souls
as we follow the path of justice,
as we look forward to signs of your love
ahead of us.
May we always know that you
and all the people of God accompany us.
Amen.

Scripture: Matthew 28:16-20

Scripture Reflection

We have been sent to teach,
preach and live your love to the world.
May we be a sign of contradiction
to those who spread fear, greed and hatred;
a sign of hope to those who are lost
and despairing;
a sign of challenge to the complacent.
May we also be witnesses to your Word.

Litany: A Cloud of Witnesses

May we be surrounded by witnesses to faith,
All: Witnesses to hope,
Witnesses to love.
With the courage of the Canadian martyrs,
All: Let us walk together;
With the compassion of St Teresa of Avila,
All: Let us walk together;
With the justice of St. Martin de Porres,
All: Let us walk together;
With the hope of the Blessed Virgin Mary,
All: Let us walk together;
With the unity of St. Paul,
All: Let us walk together;
With the wisdom of Saints Augustine and Thomas Aquinas,
All: Let us walk together;
With the perseverance of St. Vincent de Paul,
All: Let us walk together;
With the reverence of St. Francis of Assisi,
All: Let us walk together.

Closing Prayer

God of the journey,
Bless our struggling steps.
May we be supported by the many
witnesses to your love.
Forgive us when we stumble;
guide us when we lose our way;
celebrate with us when we bring joy
to the journey.
We make this prayer in the name of Jesus.
+**Amen.**

Gratitude

*O give thanks to the Lord, for he is good,
for his steadfast love endures forever.*
(Psalm 107:1)

Preparation: *Create a focal point for prayer using a Bible and traditional Thanksgiving symbols. Select readers.*

Opening Prayer

+God of life,
you knew us before we were conceived.
You wrapped us in your love
in our mother's womb.
You played with us as infants.
You sit with us in the classroom.
You watch over us when we are sick.
You welcome us with open arms when we die.
May we always give thanks for your love.
Amen.

Scripture *(based on Psalm 118:1-4)*

Give thanks to the Lord,
for God is good,
And God's love is eternal.
Let the people of God say,
All: "God's love is eternal."
Let the children of God say,
All: "God's love is eternal."
Let all who worship God say,
All: "God's love is eternal."

Scripture Reflection

It is good to be here.
May our gratitude for this moment
extend back through time,
tracing the ways of wisdom;
looking forward
with hope for promises to be fulfilled;
around the world,
to embrace your people
trying to build a Civilization of Love;
up into the heavens,
to wonder at the majesty of your creation.
May our time together remind us
of our gratitude for your gifts.
Amen.

Ritual/Litany

The community is invited to name gifts for which they are thankful. After each naming, all respond, **"We give thanks."**

Closing Prayer

Gracious God,
you bless us with many spiritual treasures:
faith, hope, love, and so many more.
May we use these gifts
to help build God's reign.
Give us grateful eyes to see your gifts
in the world.
Let this vision of the earth's beauty
give us the courage we need
to repair the brokenness
and heartbreak around us.
May God's beauty strengthen us and warm us.
We make this prayer in the name of Jesus.
+**Amen.**

God Has Compassion

*Great is your mercy, O Lord;
give me life according to your justice.*
(Psalm 119:156)

Preparation: *Place a multicoloured tablecloth, a lit candle and a Bible on your prayer table. Select readers.*

Introduction

Compassion means showing kindness
and concern for others.
Compassion means being willing
to forgive others.
Compassion means seeking to understand
others by listening to them, and doing what
we can to help those who need it.
Having compassion brings us closer to God.
Let us listen to the Word of God with
compassionate hearts.

+Scripture: Luke 10:29-37

Let us now pray to the author of our
compassionate community.
Our Father …

Compassion Quotations

1. "You may call God love, you may call God goodness. But the best name for God is compassion." (Meister Eckhart)
2. "Three things in human life are important. The first is to be kind. The second is to be kind. And the third is to be kind." (Henry James)
3. "Compassion is a two-way street." (Frank Capra)
4. "If you want others to be happy, practise compassion. If you want to be happy, practise compassion." (Dalai Lama)

Litany: Compassion

Lord, you are patient and caring.
You always find those who are lost.
**All: God has compassion for all creation.
As the cherished children of God,
we need never be afraid.**

Teach us how to forgive
so that we may live in your light.
**All: God has compassion for all creation.
Jesus paid for our sins.**

Teach us to listen attentively
so that we will not miss your call
**All: God has compassion for creation.
We need to learn how to hear with our hearts.**

Teach us all how to love
so that one day we might reach
your kingdom.
**All: God has compassion for all creation.
God brings us to light from the darkness of sin.
+Amen.**

Closing Reflection

Jesus gave us a new commandment: to love one another as he has loved us. To the family of God, compassion means celebrating our love for God's creation so our families, friends, colleagues and fellow believers know that no matter what, they can depend on us to be there for them. As we all leave here today, let us remember to share our compassion in the classroom, staffroom, home, or outside in the world of God's creation. Remember that showing compassion brings us closer to God.

Discerning Believer

I believe; help my unbelief!
(Mark 9:24)

Preparation: *In the prayer focal point, use symbols of faith such as a Bible, crucifix, candle and icon of the school's patron. Select readers.*

Opening Prayer

+God of compassion,
you created us for community.
Free us from the bonds of self-absorption.
Break down our barriers of selfishness.
Gather us together in your embrace
and give us the grace to support one another.
Guide us in our discernment,
help us to separate true faith from illusion,
and grant us wisdom and understanding.
Amen.

Scripture: Philippians 2:1-13

Blessing Prayer

Creator God,
we ask you to bless the staff and students
of this school.
May we find courage to lead our students
through their trials,
be compassionate to both friend and stranger,
seek justice where there is persecution,
find hope in moments of darkness,
seek unity when there is discord,
turn to you for wisdom in making decisions,
persevere in times of doubt and difficulty,
look with eyes of reverence upon the world,
take responsibility for our deeds, and
speak honestly even when a lie is easier.
Loving God, guide us and comfort us
through difficult times.
Challenge us to continually grow,
not only in strength, knowledge,
understanding and skill,
but also in faith, hope and love.
May we always feel your blessing upon us.
Amen.

Ritual

Each person is invited to bless their neighbour by extending their upraised hands towards them.

Litany: Living in Your Grace

God of faith,
you call us to be discerning believers.
All: Let us live in your grace.
God of faith,
you call us to create faith-filled schools.
All: Let us live in your grace.
God of faith,
you touch us through prayer, scripture,
goodness, truth and beauty.
All: Let us live in your grace.
God of faith,
you call us to celebrate the signs
of your loving presence.
All: Let us live in your grace.

Closing Prayer

Loving God,
signs of your love are all around us.
With eyes of faith we can see them.
Clear our vision,
clean our hearts,
calm our fears.
Help us draw closer to you by becoming
more discerning believers.
We make this prayer in the name of Jesus.
+**Amen.**

True Friends

A friend loves at all times.
(Proverbs 17:17)

Preparation: *Choose an area of peace and calm where there is room for all to sit or stand in a large circle. In the centre of the circle, place a prayer table with a lit candle on it. Select readers.*

Opening Prayer

+Loving Jesus,
you have called us to love one another
as you have loved us.
We thank you for your gift of friendship.
Our true friends, like you,
encourage us to hope,
strengthen our prayers,
keep our secrets,
support us in times of need,
and bless us with their love.
May we be ever thankful for our friends.
Amen.

Scripture: John 15:12-17

Litany: Friendship

**All: In true friendship,
there is complete trust.**
You can be open
with no locks on the doors to your heart.
All: There is mutual richness.
You can give and give and give
and yet gain and gain and gain.
All: There is no race or colour limitation.
All are welcome, no matter their colour,
race or creed.

**All: With a true friend
you can be yourself.**
There is no fear of ridicule or rejection.
All: Your history is an open book.
Your friend knows and accepts
where you've been.
All: Your present is not hidden.
Your friend sees and understands
where you are.
All: Your future is apparent.
Your friend acknowledges
what you will become
and encourages you to grow to your potential.

**All: A true friend is always there
to cry with you**
When you sorrow,
All: Laugh with you
When you rejoice,
All: Pray with you
When you seek spiritual guidance.

All: A true friend will hold you up
When you need support,
All: Will lean on you
When they need support,
All: Will give you wings to fly
So you can soar without fear of falling.

**All: A true friend can read your mind
with their hearts.**
They know when you mourn
All: And when you rejoice.
They know when you celebrate your successes
All: And when you endure your failures.
And they share in all these experiences
**All: Whether happy or hurtful, beneficial
or bad.**

All: True friends play the music
for your heart to dance.
Thank you, Jesus, for the gift of friends.
Amen.

Closing Prayer

Lord of friendship,
Walk beside us.
Stand with us.
Let our spirits move to the rhythm
of your love.
Open the doors to new worlds.
Engage us in new experiences.
Believe in us,
love us,
watch us soar.
Teach us to truly appreciate our friends.
We make our prayer
through our greatest friend, Jesus.
+**Amen.**

Ritual

Leader: Let us now share a sign of peace with each other.

All exchange a sign of peace.

God's Gift of Life

*[The Lord] gives breath to the people upon [the earth]
and spirit to those who walk in it.*
(Isaiah 42:5)

Preparation: *Place a lit candle and a Bible on the prayer focal point. Beside these, place images of human life, including photographs of children, graduations, marriages, school days, and items linked to prayer life (such as a rosary) and work. Select readers.*

Opening Prayer

+God of life,
we thank you for the opportunity to grow,
the chance to investigate,
and the time to discover.
Thank you for love, joy, laughter,
peace and freedom.
Thank you for the miracle of life.
We make this prayer through your Son,
Jesus Christ,
who lives and reigns with you,
one God, for ever and ever.
Amen.

Scripture: Matthew 25:14-30

Litany: God's Gift of Life

God granted us the gift of life.
God gave us breath and room to grow.
God gave us food and drink.
God gave us life.

All: In life,
God gives us complete freedom
to choose our own paths.
We can walk the well-trodden road
or blaze our own new way.
We need to take in the scenery
and record events in our memories.
These moments will not be ours again.
All: We need to keep on travelling.
We can't let life pass us by.

All: In life,
God has provided us with
one constant travelling companion.
Jesus accompanies us when we are lonely,
leads us when we are lost,
listens to us when we pray,
carries us when we fall.
All: Jesus, the true companion,
watches over us always.

All: In life,
God provides us with human company.
We may walk alone or in a large crowd;
we may decide to change
travelling companions.
All: We must choose wisely.
The people who surround us
greatly influence our lives.

All: In life,
God gives us options
about where we choose to stop.
We may wish to rest at one stage in life,
or may skip that stage altogether
and go on to another.
Not everyone stops at the same
establishments.
All: Some choose career,
some marriage, some single life.
All choices are valid.
All preferences are blessed by God.

All: In life,
God has granted us many different gifts.
We must be generous with them
and allow them to grow.
We can unwrap them at our leisure,
but we must not put them away on a shelf
or take them out only on what we deem
to be special occasions.
All: We are called to use these gifts often,
and share them.
Life is always a special occasion.

All: In life,
God allows us to gain perspective
on our journeys.
We are encouraged to live in the moment,
but we need to keep an eye
on where we are going
and keep in mind where we have been.
All: With God comes life.
With life comes time spent.
With time spent comes perspective gained.
With perspective gained
comes wisdom learned.
With wisdom learned comes truth realized.
With truth realized comes God.

All: Our life
is a journey of faith to God.
Some walk, some run;
all travel along this route.
With each passing day,
as we get closer to our final destination,
we will learn
All: Who we have been,
who we are
and who we are to become.
God has given us a precious gift;
may we not waste a moment.
All: Thank you, God, for the gift of life.
Amen.

Closing Prayer

Ever-living God,
may we continue to praise you
for the gift of life.
May we make the most of every opportunity
and savour all that life has to offer:
the joys and sorrows,
the pinnacles and valleys,
and all that lies in between.
May we grow in hope and love
on our journey of life.
+Amen.

November

Lead Us in the Footsteps of the Saints (All Saints' Day)

*They gave themselves first to the Lord and,
by the will of God, to us.*
(2 Corinthians 8:5)

Preparation: *Place several small lit candles around a large lit pillar candle on the prayer table to represent the presence of the many saints and of God. Select a reader for the Scripture and readers for "Lead Us in the Footsteps of the Saints."*

Introduction

Saints are those people who have listened to and answered God's call. They model for us that the most important part of life is showing in all that we do how much we love God, others and ourselves. Saints follow the call of the Lord, no matter what personal consequences might result. They dedicate their lives to abiding by God's Word.

+**Scripture**: Mark 12:28-34

Invitation to Prayer

No two saints are alike, just as no two people are alike. Saints do, however, share certain qualities. They hear and obey the Lord's call. They follow in the footsteps of Christ. Let us open our hearts to the will of God and follow Christ by looking to the example set by the saints.

Prayer: Lead Us in the Footsteps of the Saints

Reader 1: Nothing is unachievable when you follow God Creator or the footsteps of Jesus.
Do not let your fear or weakness stop you from doing good.
Do not let others prevent you from doing what is right.
Do not deviate from your course.
**All: O Lord our Guide,
lead us all in the footsteps of the saints.**

Reader 2: Saints do not stand idle and watch others take the lead.
They do what is needed and try their best to help others. They believe that the Gospels are not just suggestions:
rather, they are rules to live by:
feed the hungry, clothe the naked,
treat others as you would like to be treated,
and do not spread hate.
Do not be tempted to follow evil,
no matter how alluring it may seem.
**All: O Lord our Guide,
lead us all in the footsteps of the saints.**

Reader 3: We are asked to show our love to everyone we meet. For without love, our lives would be in darkness.
Saints treat everyone as their brother or sister. They see the light of Christ in every person because they hear and answer the Lord's call.
Do not paint anyone with a brush of neglect, nor close your heart to those who may be different from you.
**All: O Lord our Guide,
lead us all in the footsteps of the saints.
Amen.**

Let us all pray to our Loving God with the words Jesus has taught us.
Our Father…

Closing Prayer

God of all that is good,
We ask the help of those men and women
who have struggled against evil
and stood firm,
who loved one another,
who worked for justice and peace,
who healed the sick and fed the hungry
and who followed your Word.
Make us and all those we love
worthy to be called your saints.
We ask this through your loving Son,
Jesus Christ.
+**Amen.**

Comfort Us Today (All Souls' Day)

God will wipe away every tear from their eyes.
(Revelation 7:17)

Preparation: *For the prayer focal point, have a crucifix and a Bible as well as a lit candle. Supply small candles (tea lights or tapers) for participants to light during the Opening Prayer. You may wish to play appropriate instrumental music as the candles are being lit. Select readers.*

Opening Prayer/Ritual

+God of comfort,
God of peace,
God of love,
we bring to our hearts and minds
our loved ones who are at rest in you.
We light a candle and name our companions
who now dwell in your love.
Each person lights a candle while naming loved ones who have died.

Loving God,
bless our memories and our sorrow.
Bring comfort to those who mourn,
healing to those who doubt,
hope to those who despair.
Amen.

Scripture: John 14:1-3

Scripture Reflection

We belong in your love.
Our home is in you.
With you we discover
an end to loneliness and sorrow,
an end to discord and ugliness,
an end to selfishness and pride,
an end to deception and fear.
Comfort us with fond memories
and help us to forgive any quarrels.
Comfort us with the knowledge that
our loved ones are in peace.
Comfort us with the knowledge that
eternal rest is theirs.
Amen.

Litany: All Souls' Day

As we call to mind our loved ones
who have gone before us,
we name the many reasons why we are
thankful for their presence in our lives:
For their love for us,
All: We are thankful.
For their moments of wisdom,
All: We are thankful.
For their friendship,
All: We are thankful.
For their listening ears,
All: We are thankful.
For their times of courage,
All: We are thankful.
For the warm memories they have left with us,
All: We are thankful.

Closing Prayer

God of hope,
bless the communion we share today
with those present and with those who have
departed in your love.
May we who remain be strengthened by
their legacy of love,
so that we may live ever more faithfully
lives worthy of the name "Christian."
+**Amen.**

Choose Peace (Remembrance Day)

*He shall judge between the nations ...
nation shall not lift up sword against nation,
neither shall they learn war any more.*
(Isaiah 2:4)

Preparation: *Decorate the prayer focal point with a red tablecloth, poppies and a lit pillar candle to signify God's presence even in the face of strife. Select readers.*

Introduction: At the Last Supper, Jesus gave us the gift of peace. In today's times, we need to remember that, no matter what language we speak, the language of love and peace is universal. God gives us the responsibility of being people of peace in this wounded world. We can do this by trusting in God, listening to God, obeying God and walking with God. Let us all choose peace.

Scripture: John 14:18-20, 27

Moment of Silence

All stand to observe a moment of silence.

Leader: God our strength, help us to overcome the human obstacles we make for ourselves and make the choice for peace. We ask for the patience to deal with disagreements and the grace to live in harmony. Let us now join in a prayer that asks God to aid us with this request. We begin with the sign of the cross.

Litany: Make the Choice

All: Let us together make the choice for peace
So that together we can decide to cease hostilities among the nations.
Let us be that generation to end all wars.

All: Let us together make the choice to be friends
So that instead of seeing pain, strife and woe, we see hands of friendship extended to build new bridges between nations.
Let us strive for love and respect.

All: Let us together make the choice to help those in need
So that the poor, the sad and the lonely are not marginalized, but feel welcomed and share in the richness of our world's bounty.
Let us feed the hungry, clothe the naked and befriend the lonely.

All: Let us together make the choice for love
So that all will realize that there is only good to be gained.
The abandoned will be welcomed with open arms.
There will be
no enemies, only loved ones,
brothers and sisters in Christ.
Let us open our hearts to love one another.

All: Let us together make the choice for our Lord
So that with trust in God,
we can all live in joy and hope.
Let us praise God, who has given us life and the freedom to choose how we live it.
Let us choose peace.

**All: What a world it would be
if we lived in friendship with all nations.**
It would be a wondrous world filled with joy, love and freedom.
All: What a world it would be if no one went hungry, if there was no hatred or loneliness or want or need.
It would be a wondrous world,
filled with shared resources and mutual respect for our neighbours.

Let us, with the grace of God, make the choice to cease all hostilities and live in harmony with all nations.
All: Let us make the choice for peace.

Petitions

Loving God,
we offer you our prayers of petition.
The response is: **Lord, hear our prayer for peace.**

For all Canadian war veterans.
Let us pray to the Lord. **R.**
For all the brave soldiers who gave their lives for our freedom.
Let us pray to the Lord. **R.**
For the end to all hostilities between nations, especially war-torn regions today.
Let us pray to the Lord. **R.**
For peace in our homes, our classrooms, our schoolyards, our families, and our hearts.
Let us pray to the Lord. **R.**
For peace, support, grace and healing for those who are ill, and for those who care for them.
Let us pray to the Lord. **R.**
For those who have died, and are now at rest in God.
Let us pray to the Lord. **R.**

Ritual

Leader. Let us now share a sign of peace with each other.
All exchange a sign of peace.

Closing Prayer

God of hope,
you gave us the wonderful power to choose.
It is within our power to choose peace and not war,
to choose friendship and not fighting,
to choose love and not hatred.
We pray for your guidance to help us choose to become a people of peace.
+**Amen.**

A Vision of Justice

Do justice.
(Micah 6:8)

Preparation: *Gather in a circle to represent equality. Select readers for the Scripture and the Litany. If there are any particular justice issues that are prominent, add them to the end of the Litany using these words:*
Leader: For people affected by [name issue],
All: Open the eyes of our hearts.

Opening Prayer

+Glory to you, God our Creator …
All: Breathe into us new life, new vision.
Glory to you, God our Saviour …
All: Lead us in the way of peace and justice.
Glory to you, healing Spirit …
All: Transform us to empower others.
Amen.

Scripture: Luke 4:16-20

Reflection:

Jesus proclaims justice to the confused and to the blind. In some ways we are those people, blind to and ignorant of your goodness.
We need to allow God to open the eyes of our hearts to this vision of justice.

Litany: Justice

St. Paul wrote:
"I pray that … God … may give you a spirit of wisdom and revelation … so that, with the eyes of your heart enlightened, you may know what is the hope to which he has called you." *(Ephesians 1:17-18)*

When justice is betrayed,
All: Open the eyes of our hearts.
When sadness obscures joy,
All: Open the eyes of our hearts.
When selfishness clouds compassion,
All: Open the eyes of our hearts.
When greed blinds generosity,
All: Open the eyes of our hearts.
When resentment obliterates gratitude,
All: Open the eyes of our hearts.
When fear darkens love,
All: Open the eyes of our hearts.

All: Open the eyes of our hearts
To your Beauty,
All: Open the eyes of our hearts
To your Wisdom,
All: Open the eyes of our hearts
To your Truth,
All: Open the eyes of our hearts
To children around the world,
All: Open the eyes of our hearts
To our families,
All: Open the eyes of our hearts
To our students,
All: Open the eyes of our hearts
To our colleagues,
All: Open the eyes of our hearts
To those in our community,
All: Open the eyes of our hearts
To those in our country,
All: Open the eyes of our hearts
To all people on this planet.

Closing Prayer

God of justice,
may we always be ready
for your presence in our lives.
May we have the wisdom to see you
in the poor, the sick and the homeless.
May we always be ready
to open our hearts to you.
We make this prayer in the name of Jesus.
+**Amen.**

Ritual

Leader: Let us now share a sign of peace
and our faith with each other.
All exchange a sign of peace.

Building a Civilization of Love (Being a Responsible Citizen)

*Let love be genuine; ... hold fast to what is good;
love one another with mutual affection.*
(Romans 12:9-10)

Preparation: *Place symbols of citizenship (such as a globe, a Canadian flag, a civics textbook) in the prayer focal point. Distribute small sticky notes and pencils. Select readers.*

Opening Prayer

+Inspired by St. Teresa of Avila, we pray:
Christ's work is now our work,
Christ's hands are now our hands,
All: To wipe away a tear,
to build shelter for the homeless,
to collect food for the hungry,
to greet one another in peace.
Christ's feet are now our feet,
All: To walk along paths of justice,
to carry the load of the elderly,
to create new ways of learning
when the old ways don't work,
to lead the reluctant to freedom
and understanding.
Christ's ears are now our ears,
All: To hear the cry of the poor,
to listen to the groans of a wounded planet,
to appreciate words of wisdom and truth,
to attend to the longings and needs
of our hearts.
Christ's tongue is now our tongue,
All: To speak words of wisdom,
to teach one another
to be more than tolerant,
to correct one another
when mistakes are being made,
to speak words of forgiveness
when someone has hurt us.
Christ's mind is now our mind,
All: To remember the story
of the people of God,
to imagine a world
governed by the law of love,
to create works of beauty,
to pray in thanksgiving and
gratitude for the gifts of creation.
Christ's work is now our work.
All: Amen.

Ritual

All are invited to write on a sticky note the name of a place where God's justice and peace are sorely needed, then name it aloud as they stick the note on the globe.

Scripture: Matthew 25:31-46

Scripture Reflection

It is one thing for us to feel
a sense of responsibility,
but it is even more important for us
to take action.
May we turn
thoughts of kindness into acts of kindness;
thoughts of compassion
into deeds of compassion;
thoughts of responsibility
into works of responsibility.
In doing so, may we draw ever closer
to building a Civilization of Love.

Litany: Civilization of Love

God of justice,
architect of a Civilization of Love,
you call us to be responsible citizens.
All: Help us to follow your plan.

God of all that is good,
architect of a Civilization of Love,
you call us to give witness to goodness.
All: Help us to follow your plan.

God of peace,
architect of a Civilization of Love,
you call us to promote peace, justice
and the sacredness of human life.
All: Help us to follow your plan.

Closing Prayer

Loving God,
Jesus our teacher,
Holy Spirit of justice,
Bless the students and staff of this school.
We have answered your call
in so many ways.
Help us to continue to grow in your love.
Help us to always see you
in all the goodness of your creation.
May every step we take lead us to you.
Help us, dear God,
to live up to our responsibilities
and to help you in the building
of the Civilization of Love.
We make this prayer in the name of Jesus.
+**Amen.**

Living Water

*They did not thirst when he led them
through the deserts;
he made water flow for them from the rock.*
(Isaiah 48:21)

Preparation: *On a table, place three glass bowls of water in a large circle; one to signify God the Father, one to signify God the Son and one to signify God the Holy Spirit. In the middle of the circle, place a lit pillar candle. At the door, place another bowl of water. (Optional: Place small desktop fountains around the room.) Encourage participants to bless themselves as they enter. Select readers.*

Invitation to Prayer

Let us begin with a moment of silence,
to reflect, to focus,
to be attentive to ourselves,
to one another,
and to the presence of Christ,
who welcomes us all to share in his life.
May the Lord come and increase our faith.
Let us now welcome God's Word
into our hearts.

+**Scripture**: John 4:5-15

Litany: Let Us Drink the Living Water of Christ

Reader 1: When we drink the living water of Christ, we will never thirst.
We are sustained by his mercy and love.
We will drink and yet never thirst.
All: Let us drink the living water of Christ.
Reader 2: His Word gives us nourishment
to send down roots of faith.
Like children, we grow and thrive
in his loving care.
We will drink and yet never thirst.
All: Let us drink the living water of Christ.
Reader 3: His living water cleanses us
from our human failings.
We learn to trust his faithfulness
despite our faithlessness.
We will drink and yet never thirst.
All: Let us drink the living water of Christ.
Reader 1: His teachings give us
the courage to delve deep within ourselves,
and the will to absorb the spiritual riches
of our own stories.
We will drink and yet never thirst.
All: Let us drink the living water of Christ.
Reader 2: Let us share our stories
with the young,
for they are the future
of tomorrow and tomorrow.
Let us sustain their growth
with the living water.
Let our children grow and thrive
in Christ's loving care.
All: Let us drink the living water of Christ.
Reader 3: Let our journeys together
draw us closer to him.
Let us drink together
so that we will never thirst.
Let us drink the living water of Christ.

Let us now join in the prayer that Jesus taught us:
Our Father ...

Blessing

May Jesus fill you with new life
as you drink in his Word.
Amen.
May the faithful voices of the past
meld with those of the present
to teach the young
about our rich Christian heritage.
Amen.
May we drink the living water of Christ
so that we will never thirst,
and may God,
the Father, the Son and the Holy Spirit,
bless us.
+**Amen.**

Ritual

Leader: Let us now share a sign of peace
with each other.
All exchange a sign of peace.

What Would Jesus Do? (Social Justice)

You shall love your neighbour as yourself.
(Mark 12:31)

Preparation: *Place a lit candle on the prayer table to signify the Light of Christ in our midst. In a basket, place paper cut-outs of an open hand (one for each participant). As people enter the room, offer each one a cut-out and a pencil so they may write down one way they can help others in their community. They will bring the cut-outs to the prayer table during the petitions. Place the empty basket beside the candle on the prayer table. Select readers.*

Opening Prayer

+O Loving God,
may we your children
learn to share what we have,
offer what we can spare,
and go out and act to make this world
a friendlier, more welcoming
and comfortable place for all.
Guide us in your mercy, O Lord.
We ask this through your loving Son,
Jesus Christ.
Amen.

Scripture: Mark 10:17-21

Prayer for Social Justice

We pray for the leaders of wealthier nations,
that they may willingly share
their country's gifts
with people from poorer lands.
All: What would Jesus do?
He would act generously.
We pray for the rich,
that they may use some of their wealth
to improve the lives of the poor
and disadvantaged.
All: What would Jesus do?
He would act generously.
We pray for all of us here,
that we may not be stingy but generous
with the many gifts that God has given us.
All: What would Jesus do?
He would act generously.
We pray for the poor,
that they may have enough food and clothing
and a safe place to live and grow with dignity.
All: What would Jesus do?
He would act generously.
We pray for the powerful,
that they use their influence
to change structures
that harm the powerless.
All: What would Jesus do?
He would be a model of generosity.
Jesus is our best example
of loving generosity.
We pray that we may share what we have
with the less fortunate.
May we do what Jesus would do.
All: What would Jesus do?
Jesus would remind us that
whenever we feed, clothe
or care for another,
we follow him.
He would continue to bless us
with his abundant love.
Amen.

Participants write on their cut-outs one way they can help others in their community. During the petitions, participants bring forward their cut-outs and place them in the basket on the prayer table near the light of Christ.

Petitions

Leader: Jesus our Saviour,
we strive to follow your example
in our lives.
Bless our efforts as we pray to you.

The response is:
Help us, O Lord, to follow your example.

May we, with your inspiration
and encouragement,
answer the call to assist those
who are experiencing hardship. **R.**

May our communities
open their hearts and hands
to reach out to the needy
in our neigbourhoods. **R.**

May governments and corporations
be encouraged to set aside resources,
time and effort
to aid in global social justice. **R.**

May all of us who walk the same earth,
breathe the same air and share our world
always remember that it doesn't take much
to benefit and support others.
A smile, a helping hand,
a listening ear, a shoulder to cry on,
a shared conversation or an open mind
can make a difference. **R.**

Closing Reflection

Jesus wants all of God's wonderful gifts to be shared fairly by everyone in our world. Jesus told his disciples that the two most important commandments were to love the Lord God with all our heart, mind and soul; and to love others as ourselves. As Christians and children of God, we are called to follow the words and example of Jesus. +

Ritual

Leader: Let us now share a sign of peace with each other.
All exchange a sign of peace.

Respect the Word of the Lord

*Honour everyone. Love the family of believers.
Fear God.*
(1 Peter 2:17)

Preparation: *Place a lit pillar candle on the prayer table. Select readers.*

Opening Prayer

+God of all,
Teach us to value all life.
Implant in us a longing for mutual respect.
Kindle in us the desire to generate kindness.
Challenge us to fully appreciate all your gifts.
Encourage us in our efforts
to respect your Word.
We ask this through your Son,
our Saviour Jesus Christ.
Amen.

Scripture: Luke 10:38-42

Invitation to Prayer

Leader: In respecting the Word of God,
we come to respect ourselves, others
and all that surrounds us in life.
Let us now pray for God's grace
to rest upon each of us.

Litany: Respect

All: Respect yourself.
Sustain your bodies with all that is good.
Restore your spirit with regular prayer
**All: But above all,
respect the Word of the Lord.**

All: Respect others.
Love your neighbour, be they friend or foe.
Make sure your actions stem from love.
**All: But above all,
respect the Word of the Lord.**

All: Respect property.
Share freely of your possessions.
Handle with care the the possessions of others.
Do not take what does not belong to you.
**All: And above all,
respect the Word of the Lord**

All: Respect the world.
Respect the earth and all its riches.
The world is God's gift to us,
and it is our home.
**All: Above all, respect the Word of the Lord.
Amen.**

Let us pray in the words that Jesus taught us:
Our Father …

Closing Prayer

Father of all,
we your children are your family on earth.
Help us remain true to our calling
and to respect one another,
for in so doing, we show our respect
for the Word of the Lord.
+Amen.

December

Healing and Hope (World AIDS Day)

*Surely he has borne our infirmities
and carried our diseases.*
(Isaiah 53:4)

Preparation: *Place red ribbons with a safety pin attached (one ribbon for each person) in a basket. Distribute them as people enter the worship space, and invite people to pin on the ribbon. An AIDS awareness poster may be displayed prominently. Select readers.*

Opening Prayer

+Healing God,
bless the red ribbons we wear.
May they be a reminder
of those who live with HIV/AIDS,
of those who have died from AIDS,
of families who support those with HIV/AIDS,
of workers seeking to complete your work
of healing.
May these ribbons become signs of healing
and hope.
Amen.

Scripture: Sirach 38:1-4; 6-9

Reflection

We are called to be God's healing presence
on earth.
Today we hold close to our hearts
those of us living with HIV/AIDS.
May we all participate in God's healing
through our works of justice and charity,
through our compassion for the suffering,
through our presence among the neglected.

Litany: For Healing

Love of God,
All: Bring healing.
To those living with HIV/AIDS,
All: Bring healing.
To those who have lost a loved one to AIDS,
All: Bring healing.
To the continent of Africa,
All: Bring healing.
To grandparents caring for orphans,
All: Bring healing.
To those fighting for justice,
All: Bring healing.
To our churches, caring for the afflicted,
All: Bring healing.

Closing Prayer

Loving God,
Bless our healing hands.
Grant us wisdom and courage,
that we may advocate for the sick and dying,
that we may speak up for the widowed
and orphaned
that we may question injustices
that hinder healing.
Bless our work on your behalf.
We make this prayer in the name of Jesus
the healer.
+**Amen.**

Building Bridges Between Parents and Teachers

*Rejoice always, pray without ceasing,
give thanks in all circumstances.*
(1 Thessalonians 5:16-17)

Preparation: *For the prayer focal point, you may wish to place a picture or model of a bridge among the crucifix, Bible and candle. Select readers.*

Opening Prayer

+God of compassion,
gather us today to build bridges
between teachers and parents.
May our discussions be marked
by your wisdom and compassion,
understanding and hope.
Guide us in our meeting, so that
we may work together to raise these
precious gifts – your children.
Amen.

Scripture: Luke 2:41-52

Scripture Reflection

Can you imagine Mary's worry?
Joseph's indignation?
This story of the Holy Family is a rare
portrait of apparent dysfunction.
Do we judge the parents?
Do we blame Jesus for disobedience?
No, we look at the scene with compassion:
for the challenges parents face, and for the
challenges young people face.
Today, then, let us listen with compassionate hearts and then continue our journey
of raising loving children.

Litany: For Families

For the love of parents and children,
All: We give you thanks.
For the example of the Holy Family,
All: We give you thanks.
For the goodness of teachers in their
support of families,
All: We give you thanks.
For increased understanding between
home, parish and school,
All: We give you thanks.
For communities of caring and compassion
that make up our Catholic schools,
All: We give you thanks.

Closing Prayer

God of courage and wisdom,
We praise you and thank you
for the gifts you give your children.
May they be people of virtue.
May they know that you are with them always.
May we, as parents and teachers, teach your
goodness.
May we model a lifelong love of learning:
by showing awe at the beauty of your creation;
by showing wonder at the wisdom
of your teachings,
by gathering knowledge,
and by using this knowledge wisely.
During this school year,
bless the students in their learning,
bless the teachers in their leading,
and bless parents in their caring.
We make this prayer in the name
of Jesus the teacher.
+**Amen.**

Mary Said "Yes"

O Lord, I am your servant.
(Psalm 116:16)

Preparation: *Set the prayer table with a purple tablecloth for Advent. (If you use this prayer service at another time of year, you could use a blue cloth.) Add a vase of flowers and a lit candle. Select readers.*

Opening Prayer

+Mary, our holy mother,
you are the mother of Jesus and our mother, too.
When the Angel Gabriel told you
that God had chosen you to be the mother of his Son,
you said "yes" to the challenge.
When you knew that others around you
would question your situation,
you said "yes" to the strain.
When you had to deal with the crowds who
would gather around your Son,
you said "yes" to the effort.
We ask for your guidance as we hear
the Word of God
and try to say "yes" to what is asked of us.
For in saying "'yes," Mary, you have been forever blessed.
Amen.

Scripture: Luke 1:26-36

Litany: Mary, Our Holy Mother

Mary, you are our example of service and leadership
in accepting the Holy Spirit's gift
and becoming the Mother of Jesus.
**All: May we become leaders
and serve others
when we follow our holy mother Mary's example.**
May we answer "yes" and serve the Lord.
Mary, you were granted the Lord's grace and love,
and by these gifts you grew strong in faith and hope.
**All: May we grow stronger in faith and hope
as we follow our holy mother Mary's example.**
May we answer "yes" and serve the Lord.
Mary, in serving the Lord,
you became our caring mother
who watches over us
and whom we love and honour.
**All: May we learn to lovingly care for others
as we follow our holy mother Mary's example.**
May we answer "yes" and serve the Lord.
Mary, your soul was made glad
when you decided to follow your heart
and listen to the Word of God.
**All: May our souls be enlightened
when we follow our holy mother Mary's example.**
May we answer "yes" and serve the Lord.
Amen.

We pray for all those gathered here today,
that we may always try to do
what God asks of us.
We ask that Mary will continue to bless us
with her holy presence.
Let us pray together to our holy mother:
Hail Mary ...

Closing Reflection
Mary: A young Galilean woman betrothed
to be married.
Visited by the angel Gabriel,
a messenger from God.
Asked to bear the Son of God,
the Most High.
Understandably shocked.
Mary's faith in the Lord was so strong
that she answered "yes" to God,
though she was perplexed and afraid.
May we also be unwavering in our faith
and answer "yes" when we hear God's call.
+**Amen.**

Advent I: Hope

*Then the glory of the Lord shall be revealed,
and all people shall see it together.*
(Isaiah 40:5)

Preparation: *On the prayer table, place a purple tablecloth and an Advent wreath with one candle lit. Select readers.*

Opening Prayer

+God of hope,
we praise you during this season of Advent
and always.
Draw us into your light as we journey.
May we be filled with trust.
May our anticipation of the joyful coming
of your Son ever increase.
May our hope grow
with each passing moment.
We ask this through your Son,
our Saviour Jesus Christ.
Amen.

Scripture: Luke 3:1-17

Litany: Hope

God of hope,
your Son has shown us the way
to love ourselves, others and you.
His life has been our greatest example
of selfless love.
May our hope for the future
**All: Inspire our youth to look ahead
and grow with optimism.**
May our hope for the future
**All: Fuel our own positive outlooks
for our future endeavours.**
May our hope for the future
**All: Feed our souls with the promise of
everlasting life.**

Especially during this Advent season,
as we prepare to remember the birth
of Emmanuel,
may our hope
**All: Show us our true connection as
faithful members of God's loving family.**
May our hope
**All: Find fertile ground in us, take root,
grow and flourish throughout the world
of God's creation.**
May our hope
**All: Lead us ever closer to everlasting life
in God's kingdom**
through the love of his Son,
our Redeemer and King, Jesus Christ,
whose coming we await this Advent.
Amen.

Closing Prayer

God of hope,
As we draw ever nearer to the birth
of your Son,
Fill us with reverence as we look to the future.
Teach us to be better followers
of your Word.
May our hope be greater than yesterday,
Deepen in our hearts today,
And continue to grow beyond tomorrow.
+Amen.

Advent II: Faith

*The virgin shall conceive and bear a son,
and they shall name him Emmanuel.*
(Matthew 1:23)

Preparation: *On the prayer table, place a purple tablecloth and an Advent wreath with two candles lit. Select readers.*

Opening Prayer

+God of faith,
we praise you during this Advent season
and always.
May we walk in faith throughout our journey.
May we learn devotion from the example
of Mary.
May our faith in you grow
with each passing moment.
We ask this through your Son,
our Saviour Jesus Christ.
Amen.

Scripture: Luke 1:26-38

Litany: Faith

God of faith,
strengthen our commitment to you,
today and every day.

May our faith
**All: Teach us to recognize your grace
in our lives.**
May our faith
**All: Teach us humility and spur us on
to holiness.**
May our faith
**All: Dispel our doubts,
quench our thirst for living water
and calm our fears.**

God of faith,
especially during this Advent season
when we look forward to giving
and receiving gifts from friends and family,
help us remember that the greatest gift
we have received
is the gift of your Son Jesus.

May our faith
**All: Lead us to greater inner peace
in the hustle and bustle of this season.**
May our faith
All: Feed our hunger for the sacred.
May our faith
**All: Teach us patience as we wait
for the coming of your Son Jesus Christ.**
Mary waited for the coming of her Son
with patience and faith.
We are asked to do the same during this
and every Advent.
May we continue to grow in faith.
Amen.

Closing Prayer

Faithful God,
as we draw ever nearer to the birth
of your Son,
intensify our belief,
support our trust,
teach us to be more devoted followers
of your Word.
May our faith be greater than yesterday,
be strengthened today,
and continue to grow beyond tomorrow.
+**Amen.**

Advent III: Joy

*When they saw that the star had stopped,
they were overwhelmed with joy.*
(Matthew 2:10)

Preparation: *On the prayer table, place a purple tablecloth and an Advent wreath with three candles lit. Select readers.*

Opening Prayer

+God of joy,
we praise you during this Advent season
and always.
Fill us with gladness throughout the journey.
May we follow in the joyful steps
of the shepherds.
May we share in the jubilant song
of the angels.
May our joy grow
with each passing moment.
We ask this through your Son,
our Saviour Jesus Christ.
Amen.

Scripture: Isaiah 9:2-7

Litany: Joy

O joyful God,
you offer us relief from our inner turmoil,
freedom from life's sad moments,
and escape from darkness and deceit.
Your gift of joy opens doors to delight,
love and peace.
May our joy
**All: Open our arms to embrace
the wonders of God's creation.**
May our joy
**All: Open our eyes to recognize and fully
appreciate the simple joys that surround us.**
May our joy
**All: Open our minds to thankfully receive
and use the gifts of the Holy Spirit.**

Especially during this Advent season,
God brings peace and contentment
to those who readily see and accept
the power of God's gift of joy in our lives.

May our joy
**All: Open our hearts to offer welcome
to the coming of Emmanuel.**
May our joy
**All: Open our senses to bear witness
to the wondrous miracle of the Virgin birth.**
May our joy
**All: Open our souls to your glory
through the birth of your Son.**
May we happily walk through
your creations born of joy,
live in delight of the miracle of life
you have bestowed on us,
and express our gratitude
for the many blessings we receive each day.
Amen.

Closing Prayer

Joyful God,
As we draw nearer to the birth of your Son,
Fill us with wonder and delight.
Teach us to be better followers of your Word.
May our joy be greater than yesterday,
be strengthened today
And continue to grow beyond tomorrow.
+Amen.

Advent IV: Love

*You are my Son, the Beloved;
with you I am well pleased.*

(Luke 3:22)

Preparation: *On the prayer table, place a purple tablecloth and an Advent wreath with all four candles lit. Select readers.*

Opening Prayer

+God of love,
we praise you during this Advent season
and always.
Fill us with devotion as we journey.
May we adore you and praise your name.
May our worship translate into deep respect
for all your creation.
May our love grow with each passing moment.
We ask this through your Son,
our Saviour Jesus Christ.
Amen.

Scripture: Luke 1:39-45

Litany: Love

God of love,
your Son has shown us the way
to love ourselves, to love others,
and to love you.
His life is our greatest example of selfless love.

May our love for ourselves
**All: Be a sign of gratitude for the gift
of life, enriched and blessed every day
by the grace of your presence.**
May our love for others
**All: Be a reward for answering your call
to follow the greatest commandment
of your Son.**
May our love for you
**All: Be a sign of our complete trust
in the Trinity:
reverence for God the Father,
devotion for God the Son,
and deep faith in God the Holy Spirit.**

Especially during this Advent season,
as we prepare to welcome Emmanuel,
may God's love for us
**All: Show us the true connection we share
as faithful members of God's loving family.**
May God's love for us
**All: Find fertile ground in us,
take root, grow and flourish
throughout the world of God's creation.**
May God's love for us
**All: Lead us ever closer to everlasting life
in God's kingdom
through the love of his Son,
our Redeemer and King, Jesus Christ,
whose coming we await with love this Advent.
Amen.**

Closing Prayer

Loving God,
as we draw nearer to the birth of your Son,
guide us in our worship.
Teach us to be better followers of your Word.
May our love be greater than yesterday,
increase today,
and continue to grow beyond tomorrow.
+**Amen.**

Preparing for Christmas

A voice cries out:
"In the wilderness prepare the way of the Lord."
(Isaiah 40:3)

Preparation: *On your prayer table, place a purple tablecloth and an Advent wreath with the appropriate number of candles lit depending on the week of Advent. Select readers.*

Opening Prayer

+Loving God,
today we gather together as friends
and co-workers
to celebrate the coming birth of your Son,
Jesus Christ our Saviour.
At times during this season of Advent,
we are too focused on
shopping, cooking, and
keeping commitments with family and
friends.
Help us to remember
amid all the hustle and bustle
that Jesus is the true gift of Christmas.
Amen.

Scripture: Luke 3:10-11, 14-16

Scripture Reflection

We are called to love others.
We are called to share of ourselves.
We are called to be disciples of Christ.
We are called to follow Jesus.
Jesus is the true gift of Christmas.

Litany: The True Gift of Christmas

Christmas is the time of love, peace, hope and goodwill.
So why do we push and shove in lines at the shopping mall?
Why are we impatient in the parking lot?
All: Jesus is the true gift of Christmas.
Christmas is the time to share a meal
and conversation with those we love.
Wouldn't it be wonderful if we also thought
of the friendless and the lonely?
All: Jesus is the true gift of Christmas.
Christmas is the time for turkey, stuffing,
plum puddings, eggnog and wonderful desserts.
Yet do we share our abundance with those
people in our communities who do not have
enough to eat?
All: Jesus is the true gift of Christmas.
Open your hearts first, not your bags.
Think of others first, not of yourselves.
For Christmas is the birthday of Jesus.
It does not matter what presents
we can afford,
Because…
Jesus is the true gift of Christmas.
Amen.

Closing Prayer

Loving God,
we are all servants of Christ.
Help us to remember amid the busy preparations
for visiting with friends and family
that in everyone, rich or poor,
and in every time, joyous or solemn,
you are there.
We ask this through your Son,
our Saviour Jesus Christ.
+**Amen.**

January

New Beginnings (New Year)

If you have been raised with Christ, seek the things that are above, where Christ is.
(Colossians 3:1)

Preparation: *Place a white tablecloth, a Bible and a white pillar candle on the prayer table. White signifies newness or starting afresh; a lit candle represents the presence of God. As participants enter, give them a slip of paper and a pencil. During the reflection time, they can jot down their answers to the questions. Select readers.*

Invitation to Prayer

The new year is the time of new beginnings.
We begin with new resolutions,
start a new term,
renew old acquaintances,
and make a fresh start.

+Scripture: Ephesians 5:14-20

Litany: Let us Renew our Faith

It is the New Year
and time for a new beginning.
It is time to show a change of heart
and clear out the cobwebs of sin.
**All: Let us renew our faith.
Let us refresh our vow.**
For it is in remembering
the solemn promise of our ancestors
that we should always awaken
with words of praise to God on our lips.
**All: Let us renew our faith.
Let us refresh our vow.**
For it is our allowing God to guide us in all
we say and do in our lives
that will assure our happiness
and the glory of our God.
**All: Let us renew our faith.
Let us refresh our vow.**
So, in the coming days, weeks and months,
Let us rekindle our love of the Spirit,
our Creator and his Son.
**All: Let us renew our faith.
Let us refresh our vow.**
It is the New Year
and time for a fresh beginning.
We will clear the taint of sin
from our hearts, with God's help.
**All: Let us renew our faith.
Let us refresh our vow.**

God of Newness,
bless this new year.
Help us to learn from the mistakes of yesteryear and begin this year with a clean heart.
As we make our individual promises to you,
help us to fulfill our oaths.
Give us the strength to persevere
and maintain a true course.
Amen.

All answer the reflection questions below using the paper and pencil they were given. (They will take their answers with them; no one will read what they write.)

Reflection

Allow a minute or two between each question.

- What would you like to improve in yourself this term (personally, professionally)?
- What can you do to improve the world around you?
- What can you do to improve your relationships with friends or others?
- How do these changes bring you closer to God?

Closing Prayer

God of all that is good,
As we leave here today with promises in hand,
watch over us
and strengthen our resolve
in times of weakness.
Though we all have the best of intentions,
it is often hard to reach the ideals
we set for ourselves.
Guide us in our struggles;
encourage us in our attempts;
keep us ever stretching to reach our goals,
for it is in the struggle
that we grow closer to you.
We ask this through your loving Son,
Jesus Christ.
+**Amen.**

To Be Your People (Epiphany)

*On entering the house, they saw the child
with Mary his mother.*
(Matthew 2:11)

Preparation: *For the prayer focal point, a crèche is appropriate. Fill a basket with pebbles (one for each person) for the ritual. On each pebble write the name of a different gift, such as peace, hope, love, joy, courage. Select readers.*

Opening Prayer

+In this place, in this new year,
we become quiet and still
in the presence of the sacred.
Loving God,
you understand the need to be quiet
amid the bustle of life.
Bring peace into our souls,
and let all we do in this gathering
be done in love.
We ask this in the name of Jesus,
the Prince of Peace.
Amen.

Ritual

Participants come forward, one at a time, and choose a pebble from the basket. They consider the gift written on the pebble and think about how they can give this gift back to God.

Scripture: Matthew 2:1-12

Scripture Reflection

Gracious God,
any gifts we give are but a distant echo
of your original gifts of love.
Nevertheless, we bring them before you.
Bless and nurture our offerings:
our trust and our faith,
our optimism and our hope,
our affection and our love.
Like the wise men who visited the stable,
we humbly offer you our gifts.

Litany: Gifts of the Heart

Creator God,
you bless us with gifts of creation.
All: May we always be thankful.
Divine Teacher,
you bless us with wisdom and truth.
All: May we always learn by your side.
Lover of Humanity,
you bless us with compassion and kindness.
All: May we always respect one another.
Servant Leader,
you bless us by teaching peace and justice.
All: May we always serve those in need.

Closing Prayer

Loving God,
we thank you for all your gifts to us.
This new year,
we give you thanks for all the good things
you have done for us.
We thank you for all who share in the work
of our schools this year,
and ask you to bless us all with your love.
We make this prayer in the name of the
Prince of Peace.
+**Amen.**

The Season of Winter

As I looked, a stormy wind came out of the north.
(Ezekiel 1:4)

Preparation: *On your prayer centre, place a white tablecloth and a large plate. In the centre of the plate, place a lit white pillar candle. Divide participants into two groups. Have representatives from each groups add pine cones and evergreen sprigs to the plate during the Litany. Select readers.*

Opening Prayer

+God of the seasons,
you bless us with the cold beauty of winter.
you call us to awaken to a world
blanketed in white.
you call us to see similarities
between the mighty oak and the small sapling;
between the large mansion
and the small home;
between peoples of different nations.
You call us to see that we are one:
one with each other,
one with nature,
one with you.
Help us to appreciate
the many wonders of our world.
We ask this through your Son, Jesus Christ.
Amen.

Scripture: Job 36:5-6, 9-12

Litany: Winter

Group 1: To the north, to the east,
to the south, to the west,
Leader: No matter where we are
during the season of winter,
we see that God shows us
the wonders of our world,
the glory of creation,
the splendours of life.
Group 2: Inward, outward and all around us,
Leader: At every turn and within our hearts,
we feel God's great love for us.
With every crisp breath
and with every glance around us,
we see the presence of God.
**All: For God graces us children
with the season of winter.**

Leader: God blesses us
with myriad snowflakes,
Group 1: Icy cold weather
where everything freezes,
Group 2: Glacial, diamond-like, icy rooms,
Group 1: Brisk, clear days and fluffy snow
like soapsuds,
Group 2: Sparkling, crystalline icicles
in every cranny and nook.
Group 1: From the north, from the east,
from the south, from the west,
Leader: No matter where we look,
and at every turn,
**All: God graces us children
with the season of winter.**

Closing Prayer

God of the seasons,
may we learn to acknowledge and embrace
the differences between us and our neighbours
during this winter season.
May our sharing of this world
during these winter months
lead us to share our souls,
share our faith journey,
and share peace.
+**Amen.**

In God's Time

Be careful then how you live, not as unwise people but as wise, making the most of the time.
(Ephesians 5:15)

Preparation: *At the centre of the prayer table, place various timepieces, such as a clock, a watch, an hourglass, a stop watch. Light a candle and place it in the middle of these items to signify God's presence at all times in our lives. As people arrive, give them a pencil and a small slip of paper. Ask them to write down three or four things they need to do but feel they don't have time for. Have them to fold their paper, and put their name on the outside, and place it around the timepieces. Assure them that no one else will read it; they will retrieve it themselves later in the service. Select readers.*

Opening Prayer

+We have been given the gift of time:
a whole year
to make a difference
in the lives of other people.
A whole year
to grow in faith.
A whole year
to make peace and justice a reality.
A whole year
to create, to love, to grow.

Thank you, God, for this gift of time.
Help us to use it wisely and to remember
that the gift of this time comes but once.
Amen.

Scripture: Ecclesiastes 3:1-8

Prayer for Time

The response is: **It is time to begin,
time to learn, time to love, time to pray.**

Eternal God, it is time to begin.
It is time to continue.
It is time to end.
Our time on this world is finite.
Your time is infinite.
Help us to use our time wisely. **R.**

Eternal God, it is time to learn.
Help us to distinguish between
the tasks we think are important
and the tasks that really have meaning.
Help us to use our time
to complete all that you set out for us.
Help us to use our time wisely. **R.**

Eternal God, it is time to love.
Help us to use our time and talents
to help, teach and serve others.
For it is during this time
that we show our love and best serve you.
Help us to use our time wisely. **R.**

Eternal God, it is time to pray.
Help us to use our time
to praise you in thanksgiving,
to thank you for our many blessings,
to worship you with reverence,
to humbly ask your forgiveness when we fall.
Help us to use our time wisely. **R.**
All: **There is time to do all that you ask of us.
May we learn to listen to your will
with faithful and willing hearts.
May we learn to use our time wisely.
Amen.**

Reflection

Invite participants to retrieve their slip of paper from the prayer centre.

Leader: Think about what you have written on your slip of paper. Then ask yourself the following questions:

- Do these tasks that I have set out for myself serve others, God, or me?
- Are there some tasks that I don't really need to do?
- Will completing these tasks be a good use of my time?
- How can I set realistic priorities?

Allow a few minutes for all reflect on the questions.

The gift of time is ours today. Remember that this precious gift flies faster and faster with each passing year. Don't let the gift of time pass you by.

Let us join in praying the prayer that Jesus taught us.
All: Our Father …

Closing Prayer

Eternal God,
teach us to use our time wisely.
Help us to remember
that in order to be the hands and feet
and eyes of your Son Jesus,
we must use our time and efforts to pray,
to help and teach others,
and to share our talents with those around us.
But we must also remember to make time
for ourselves.
Without it, we lack the energy to reach out
and fulfill our calling.
Without it, we are not healthy or happy.
Teach us, Lord, to use your gift
of time wisely.
We ask this through your Son, Jesus Christ,
who lives and reigns with you,
one God for ever and ever.
+**Amen.**

We Are United in Christ

All of you are one in Christ Jesus.
(Galatians 3:28)

Preparation: *Place a lit candle on the prayer table to symbolize the presence of God. Arrange chairs in a large circle to represent unity. Select readers.*

Opening Prayer

+Jesus our Lord,
may we find our way to you,
where all are welcome,
all are loved and respected,
and all are valued members of God's family.
May we live our lives on earth in unity,
welcoming all,
loving and respecting all,
and valuing all as children of God.
Amen.

Scripture: 1 Corinthians 12:12-27

Litany: Let us Live in Unity

We are called to welcome the stranger
as sincerely as our friend.
We are called to serve our neighbour
with joyful and generous hearts.
All: Let us live in unity.
Let us live in you.
We are called to love our enemies
as warmly as our family and friends.
We must open up our hearts
and let the Spirit in,
forgiving those who have wronged us.
All: Let us live in unity.
Let us live in you.
We are called to always keep in mind
that we are all the children of God.
We need to model Jesus
by following in his footsteps.
So let us journey together.
All: Let us live in unity.
Let us live in you.
God calls us each by name.
Jesus loved all people,
blind or ill or poor.
In gladly accepting all people,
we can begin afresh,
All: And all will live in unity.
All will live in you. Amen.

Let us pray the words that Jesus taught us:
Our Father ...

Closing Prayer

God of unity,
help us to live our lives
unified under the banner of Christ,
for it is through his eyes
that we see your true glory.
We ask this through your Son, Jesus Christ.
+Amen.

Being a Collaborative Contributor (Collaboration)

*Iron sharpens iron,
And one person sharpens the wits of another.*
(Proverbs 27:17)

Preparation: *On the prayer focal point, place a tablecloth in a colour appropriate to the liturgical season. Arrange chairs in a circle around the focal point. Select readers.*

Opening Prayer

+God of unity,
you call us to work together
to bring healing to the hurting.
Touch our hands,
that we use them for blessing, not harming.
Touch our hearts,
that we use them for joining, not parting.
Touch our minds,
that we use them for harmony, not discord.
Amen.

Scripture: Romans 12:4-10

Scripture Reflection

Loving God,
you created us uniquely gifted.
Within us is the call to love,
the call to live out of your love,
the call to bring your love into service.
May each of us discover our own gifts
and use them to help build your kingdom.
May we respect each other's gifts
and help each other to grow in our giftedness.
Bless us with listening hearts
and compassionate actions.

Litany: The Gift of Community

As each prayer is offered, picture someone in the community who reflects this gift.
For the wise,
All: We give thanks.
For the patient,
All: We give thanks.
For the gracious,
All: We give thanks.
For the creative,
All: We give thanks.
For the visionaries,
All: We give thanks.
For the humble,
All: We give thanks.
For the diligent,
All: We give thanks.
For the careful,
All: We give thanks.
For the listeners,
All: We give thanks.
For the articulate,
All: We give thanks.
For the truth-tellers,
All: We give thanks.
For the reflective,
All: We give thanks.
For the joyful,
All: We give thanks.
For the dreamers,
All: We give thanks.
For the practical,
All: We give thanks.
For the kind,
All: We give thanks.
For the organized,
All: We give thanks.

For the hopeful,
All: We give thanks.
For the reverent,
All: We give thanks.
For us all,
All: We give thanks.

Ritual

Leader: As a sign of unity,
we join our hands together
to pray the Our Father,
a prayer that unites Christians
through time and space.
All: Our Father …

Closing Prayer

God of unity,
when your wisdom reigns in our community,
your communion harmonizes our differences.
Bless us with understanding
so that we may better live
your dream of unity.
We make this prayer in the name of Jesus.
+**Amen.**

The True Nature of God (St. Thomas Aquinas)

*I am the first and I am the last;
besides me there is no god.*
(Isaiah 44:6)

Preparation: *Place a lit candle and a Bible on the prayer table. Add an icon or pictures of St. Thomas Aquinas, if available. Select readers for the Litany and the scripture reading.*

Introduction

Today we celebrate St. Thomas Aquinas, patron saint of Catholic schools and students. Thomas was born to a wealthy family in Italy around the year 1225. He was highly intelligent, but because he was large and very quiet, many called him "the dumb ox." His family intended that Thomas, as befitted his station in life, would become abbot of the Benedictine monastery after his uncle left the prestigious position. Thomas, however, wanted desperately to become a Dominican priest. The Dominicans' vow of poverty and simple lifestyle of prayer set his family against this. They imprisoned him in the family castle for a year, hoping to dissuade him from this course, but he remained steadfast. When they finally released him, he did indeed become a Dominican priest. During his life, Thomas refused many offers to advance his career, because he felt that God was calling him to write and pray. He put his life completely into the Lord's hands. Thomas wrote many books on Christianity, including his masterpiece, the *Summa Theologica*. His writings are hailed by Christian scholars around the world.

Opening Prayer

+God our strength,
Help us to be more like the saints
who show us that what matters most in life
is not what we own,
or who we know,
or the job we do;
what matters is how much faith,
love and trust we have in God,
and how well we show these in all we do.
Help us to learn that there are many ways
to follow Christ.
Amen.

Scripture: 1 Thessalonians 5:12-24

Litany: The True Nature of God

Thomas believed and wrote that the nature of God could be described in five simple statements. Let us use these as a framework to pray.
"God is simple, without composition of parts, body matter or form."
Reader 1: God, in his simplicity, loves us, his fragile children.
One day our bodies will fail,
but we will rejoice
because we can then live eternally
with God our Father.
All: Only then will we begin to understand the perfect simplicity that is God.

Leader: *"God is perfect and lacks nothing."*
Reader 2: We cannot begin to comprehend the perfection of God.
Some see perfection in the tiny features of newborn babies.

71

For others, a lovely sunset
or the call of a loon
approaches the ideal for beauty.
We will rejoice
when we live with God eternally.
**All: Only then will we experience
God's perfect nature.**

Leader: *"God is infinite in that God has no physical, emotional or intellectual limits."*
Reader 3: God loves us even though we exist
within our limited human condition.
We have been formed in God's image
and have been given the precious gift of life.
Yet we cannot imagine a limitless existence.
We cannot imagine life without bounds.
We will rejoice
when we are invited to God's kingdom.
**All: Only then will we comprehend
God's infinite existence.**

Leader: *"God is immutable. No changes will ever alter the essence of God."*
Reader 4: God always was, always is,
and always shall be.
We find comfort in this knowledge.
For our bodies grow older every moment,
we change every day,
and our lives on this earth are finite.
God, however, remains unchanged.
God's love for us is steadfast.
We will rejoice
when we are invited to reside with God
in heaven.
**All: Only then will we fully understand
that God is immutable.**

Leader: *"God is One. There is no other. The Trinity forms the essence of God."*
Reader 5: There is only one God
who exists for us in the form of the Trinity,
three persons in one: God the Father,
God the Son and God the Holy Spirit.
All possess the divine nature that is God.
All form the essential essence that is God.
Truly we will rejoice
when we see our God face to face.
**All: Only then will we fully understand
the Oneness of God.
God is simple, perfect, infinite
and immutable, and God is One.
Thanks be to God.
Amen.**

Closing Prayer

God our Creator,
help us to be more like St. Thomas Aquinas.
Teach us to put our trust in you, as he did.
Lead us in our search for truth.
May St. Thomas and all the saints
guide our steps in goodness,
befriend us in loneliness,
and strengthen us in danger.
+Amen.

We Believe

I know the one in whom I have put my trust.
(2 Timothy 1:12)

Preparation: *Place a lit candle and a Bible on the prayer table. Select readers.*

Introduction

Faith means believing in something even though we haven't seen it. Faith isn't based on logic or scientific data. Our belief is rooted in the certain knowledge that we are all the cherished children of God. Our faith allows us to know with all our hearts and with every fibre of our being that we can trust in God's unending love for us. God is always there in every moment of sorrow, triumph, joy and despair. We know this simply because we believe.

Opening Prayer

+Ever-faithful God,
we know that you are with us
from the moment of our conception.
We know that you are with us
in every breath we take.
We know that you are with us
at the hour of our death and beyond.
Strengthen our faith in you,
that we may draw ever closer
to your heavenly kingdom.
We ask this through your Son, Jesus Christ,
who lives and reigns with you,
One God for ever and ever.
Amen.

Scripture: John 20:19-29

Prayer: We Believe in you Our Lord

We have spent all of our lives believing
that the world is what our senses reveal to us.
Our experience is what we see, hear, feel,
taste and smell.
So, then, what do we believe in
when we kneel?
All: We believe in you, our Lord.

**All: We believe in you, Lord,
though we do not see your form
with our eyes.**
We see you in the faces of those we love
and in the beauty of a sunset.
**All: We believe in you, Lord,
though we do not listen with our ears
to hear your voice.**
We hear you call us in our hearts and souls
and in the cry of a newborn.
**All: We believe in you, Lord,
though we do not taste your presence
with our tongue.**
We taste the sweet nectar of life's pleasures
in our youth and when we are older.
**All: We believe in you, Lord,
though we do not sense your presence
with our nose.**
We sense you in the perfume of the blooms
and blossoms that grow in our gardens.
**All: We believe in you, Lord,
though we do not feel
your physical touch.**
We feel the caress of the gentle breezes
you send, and feel the warmth of the sun.
**All: We believe in you without seeing,
hearing, tasting, smelling or touching.**

You are ever present to us in every moment of our lives. We do not even need to use our senses to know that you are there.
All: We believe in you, our Lord. Amen.

Let us pray to the one in whom we believe, in the words Jesus has taught us:
All: Our Father ... +

Closing Reflection

We recognize the hand of God in everything good in our lives. We do not need to see, hear, taste, smell or feel God physically to know God is there. We just know. We know God supports us in times of need, rejoices with us in times of joy, and nurtures us in times of doubt. We have faith in Jesus, the Risen Christ. We believe.

February

Sowing the Seeds of Your Love (New Semester)

The sower sows the word.
(Mark 4:14)

Preparation: *On the prayer focal point, place seeds or packets of seeds, a bowl of crystal salt, a candle and a Bible. Select readers.*

Opening Prayer

+God of wisdom and hope,
you call us to work in your fields,
to sow the seeds of your love,
to weed out injustice,
to nurture the young and the needy.
May we answer this call with humility,
trust and joy.
May we always know
that you are working with us.
May we always know your comfort
and support.
Amen.

Scripture: Mark 1:14-20

Rite of Commissioning

Leader: Beloved disciples of Christ,
we once again commission you
as educators and ministers.
You have been called to serve
the young, the blessed children of God.
All: **We are called to act justly,
love tenderly,
and walk humbly with our God.**
Leader: As teachers in our Catholic schools,
may you be nurtured and blessed,
may you be honoured and loved,
may you be inspired and inspiring.
All: **We are blessed
and we will pass on this blessing.**
Leader: God grant you wisdom
for the journey,
love in your meetings,
hope in your partings,
joy in your greetings.
All: **We ask for this grace in the name
of Jesus.**

Closing Prayer

Loving God, master teacher,
Spirit of wisdom,
as Catholic teachers,
we pray for the students entrusted to us
in our school.
Help us to teach our children
to walk in your ways.
Help us to support home and parish
in raising young women and men
to be people of prayer, love,
integrity and justice.
Bless our students in their lifelong
pilgrimages towards heaven.
Bless us in assisting them on their paths.
We make this prayer in the name of Jesus
the teacher.
+**Amen.**

Let Us Celebrate Our Differences

Everyone who calls on the name of the Lord shall be saved.
(Acts 2:21)

Preparation: *Place lit candles of different colours and sizes around a larger pillar candle to represent all of God's children sharing in his Light. Select readers.*

Invitation to Prayer

We all look different on the outside, but on the inside we are all members of the family of God. In every faith, people bless their participation in the natural world around them. In spite of or even because of our differences, we are all loved. No matter what our faith, colour, race, age or gender, we are all cherished as God's children. Let us now listen to God's Word.

+**Scripture**: Galatians 3:27-29

Litany: Let Us Celebrate Our Differences

Let us celebrate our differences.
Let us rejoice in the endless array of human-kind
for we are all children of God.
**All: Let us relish God's infinite variety
and celebrate our differences.**
We are Black, White, Aboriginal, Asian, Indian.
We are Muslim, Hindu, Buddhist,
Jewish, Catholic.
We are men, women, teenagers,
children, infants.
We are all children of God.
**All: Let us relish God's infinite variety.
Let us celebrate our differences.**
We are rich; we are poor.
We live in mansions; we live in huts.
We eat every day; we are starving.
Yet we all pray to the One Most High,
for we are all children of God.
**All: Let us relish God's infinite variety.
Let us celebrate our differences.**
Let us not be strangers,
but loving citizens of faith.
Let us grow in the knowledge
that we are precious in God's sight,
for we are children of God.
**All: Let us relish God's infinite variety.
Let us celebrate our differences.**
We are different faiths.
We are different colours.
We are different races.
We speak different languages.
Yet we seek one truth,
for we are all children of God.
**All: Let us relish God's infinite variety.
Let us celebrate our differences,
for we are all children of God.
Amen.**

Closing Prayer

Ever-loving God,
With sincere hearts and open minds,
may we always embrace differences
in each other,
celebrate the infinite variety of humanity,
and share in the diverse life experiences
that you send us.
We ask this through Jesus Christ, our brother.
+**Amen.**

Let Us Praise Wisdom

*Happy are those who find wisdom ...
for her income is better than silver,
and her revenue better than gold.*
(Proverbs 3:13-14)

Preparation: *In the focal prayer space, place a lit candle, Bible and a crucifix or cross. Select readers.*

Opening Reflection
(adapted from Wisdom 6:12-16)

Let us praise Wisdom
as personified in the Hebrew Scriptures:
Wisdom is radiant and unfading.
She is easily discerned by those who love her,
and is found by those who seek her.
She runs to make herself known
to those who desire her.
One who rises early to seek her
will have no difficulty,
for she will be found sitting at the gate.
To fix one's thought on her
is perfect understanding,
and one who is vigilant on her account
will soon be free from care,
because she goes about seeking
those worthy of her,
and she graciously appears to them
in their paths,
and meets them in every thought.

Ritual

Each participant names a saint or other person who exemplifies wisdom. After the person is named, all respond: **Walk with us.**

Scripture: Matthew 5:13-16

Scripture Reflection

Reader 1: God of wisdom,
you know that we love you.
You know we want to be salt and light.
But the task is tiring and at times lonely.
Help us and be near us.

Reader 2: Be still.
Be quiet like the oak tree.
Be at rest; be at peace.
You are rooted in deep soil
that is rich in nutrition with plenty of water.

Reader 1: Loving God,
teach me to be still,
to hear your voice,
to feel your Wisdom flowing through me,
to be at home with you.

Litany: Wisdom

Make our hearts full of thanks for your love.
All: Wisdom, flow through us.
Make our learning full of joy.
All: Wisdom, flow through us.
Help our minds grow in understanding.
All: Wisdom, flow through us.
Touch our souls with compassion.
All: Wisdom, flow through us.
Guide our feet to walk in your ways.
All: Wisdom, flow through us.
Help our hands create a loving world.
All: Wisdom, flow through us.

Closing Prayer

Reader 1: Spirit of wisdom,
All: Send truth to correct deception.
Reader 2: Spirit of wisdom,
All: Send humility to temper authority.
Reader 1: Spirit of wisdom,
All: Send patience to harness haste.
Reader 2: Spirit of wisdom,
All: Send hope to proclaim an end to despair.
Reader 1: Spirit of creativity,
All: Send imagination to play with experience.
Reader 2: Spirit of creativity,
All: Send possibility to dance with practicality.
Reader 1: Spirit of creativity,
All: Send vision to converse with tradition.
Reader 2: Spirit of creativity,
All: Send insight that leads to action.
Reader 1: Spirit of reflection,
All: Send quiet into our hurry.
Reader 2: Spirit of reflection,
All: Send love into our decisions.
Reader 1: Spirit of reflection,
All: Send gratitude into our remembrance.
Reader 2: Spirit of reflection,
All: Send faith into all we do.
Reader 1: We make this prayer through our brother Jesus.
Amen.

God's Love for Us

Whoever obeys [Christ's] word, truly in this person the love of God has reached perfection.
(1 John 2:5)

Preparation: *Place a red tablecloth on your prayer table, or decorate your prayer space with hearts. Place a lit candle on the prayer table. Select readers.*

Opening Prayer

+God our loving Father,
you have loved us from before our first breath.
You gave up your only Son for us as a sign of your love.
May we your children ever praise you with devotion.
Amen.

Scripture: 1 John 4:7-21

Prayer of Love

Patience is born of wisdom:
All: **Though human impatience is our failing,**
God's wisdom will guide us to patience.
Acceptance is born of faith:
All: **Though humanity struggles to accept all peoples,**
God's faith will guide us to acceptance.
Hope is born of trust:
All: **Though humanity loses hope in the face of doubt,**
God's trust will guide us to hope.
Forgiveness is born of sincerity:
All: **Though humanity looks for forgiveness,**
God's sincerity will guide us to forgiveness.
Life is born of love:
All: **Though human love is bounded by the limits of our lives,**
God's love will guide us to life in him.
God's love for us is eternal.
God's love for us has no bounds.
God's love is born of wisdom, faith, trust and sincerity.
God's love leads us to patience, acceptance, hope and forgiveness.
All: **God's love gives us room to grow and wings to fly.**
Blessed are we, who receive the love of God.
Blessed are we, the cherished children of God.
Amen.

Closing Prayer

Loving God,
It is you who tenderly watches over your Creation.
It is you who loved us from our earliest moments.
It is you who taught us how to love.
It is you who will eternally love us beyond the grave.
Thank you, Lord, for your everlasting love.
+**Amen.**

God Will Be There

"I am the Alpha and the Omega," says the Lord God, who is and who was and who is to come.
(Revelation 1:8)

Preparation: *On the prayer focal point, place a cloth in the colour of the liturgical season, a lit pillar candle and a Bible. You will need six tapers for the ritual for the Litany and six people to light the tapers. Select readers.*

Opening Prayer

God of all eternity,
you always were, always are,
and always will be.
Your love for us is infinite.
Before we were thought of,
before we were born,
you smiled on us as your beloved children.
May we always remember that in all things,
you will be there.
Amen.

Scripture: Isaiah 44:6-8

Litany/Ritual: God Will Be There

During this Litany, six people each light a taper from the pillar candle at the prayer focal point to signify God's presence in the light among and around us. As each taper is lit, all respond: **God will be there.**

When we embrace God's love;
when we are kind to all our sisters
and brothers in Christ,
All: God will be there.
When we fall into sin or when we fail;
when we are ill or when we are healthy,
All: God will be there.
When we soar to the greatest of heights;
when we experience life's true joys,
All: God will be there.
When we are in pain or lonely;
when the sun doesn't seem likely
to shine again,
All: God will be there.
When we endure our deepest sorrow
and grief;
when life seems to take away
our tomorrows,
All: God will be there.
When we reach the end of our lives,
we remember that God has been waiting
for us since our birth:
All: God will be there.
Amen.

Let us now pray to our eternal God
in the words that Jesus taught us:
Our Father …

Closing Prayer

God our Creator,
we praise you for the infinite nature
of your love for us.
We revere you for gracing us with life.
We thank you for bestowing countless
blessings on us.
We make this prayer through Jesus Christ,
our Eternal Brother.
Amen. +

Lead Us into the Desert (Ash Wednesday)

O give thanks to the Lord ... who led his people through the wilderness.
(Psalm 136:1, 16)

Preparation: *At the focal point of the prayer space, place the ashes on a purple tablecloth. Select readers.*

(Note: The usual place for receiving ashes is at your parish. This prayer service is intended to be used when attending the parish celebration is not possible.)

Opening Prayer

+God of the desert,
lead us once more along wilderness paths.
Lead us through the dry places in our hearts,
where faith has gone stale,
where forgiveness is forgotten,
where hope has turned to despair,
where joy has become fear.
May we water those places with your love
to make our desert hearts bloom again,
so we can become living gospels,
living testaments to your ways.
Amen.

Scripture: Mark 1:12-15

Litany: Our Lenten Journey

God of the journey,
lead us this Lent into the desert,
where we fast on simplicity,
and to the oasis, where we feast
on your companionship.
May we fast from anger
All: And feast on reconciliation.
May we fast from selfishness
All: And feast on generosity.
May we fast from resentment
All: And feast on gratitude.
May we fast from fear
All: And feast on courage.
May we fast from self-absorption
All: And feast on compassion.
May we fast from exploitation
All: And feast on justice.
May we fast from despair
All: And feast on hope.
May we fast from antagonism
All: And feast on unity.
May we fast from foolishness
All: And feast on wisdom.
May we fast from weakness
All: And feast on perseverance.
May we fast from distraction
All: And feast on reverence.
May we fast from recklessness
All: And feast on responsibility.
May we fast from deception
All: And feast on honesty.

Loving God,
may our Lent be a holy preparation.
May our preparation be blessed
and never finished
until we rest completely in you.
Amen.

Silence

Participants are silent in preparation for the distribution of ashes. You may wish to read aloud the following reflection at this time.

Reflection

High above the desert,
the wind chases sand into clouds.
From this rock I can see
the choking dust swirl,
and then settle on the path,
obscuring the way.

Along the route comes an old woman
with a broom.
On this desert morning
she sweeps the pathway clear
so her children can find their way home.
I follow her example
and sweep the paths of my life,
although I know that this path
leads to Gethsemane and beyond.
Because I know that this path
leads to Gethsemane and beyond.

Ritual

Distribution of ashes (follow diocesan norms)

Closing Prayer

Spirit of simplicity,
bless our community.
Lead us with wisdom and perseverance
on our Lenten journey.
Bless us as we clear our paths to your love.
Bless the marks on our foreheads;
may they be a sign of fasting from fear
and feasting on love.
We make this prayer in the name of Jesus.
+**Amen.**

Desert, Teach Me (Prayers for Reconciliation)

*As far as the east is from the west,
so far he removes our transgressions from us.*
(Psalm 103:12)

Preparation: *Place a purple tablecloth on the prayer focal point. Partially fill a clear glass bowl with sand to represent the desert and place it on the purple cloth. Select readers.*

Opening Prayer

+God of love,
there are times when our hearts are broken by division:
when we are at odds with our deepest selves,
our family and friends,
our community,
even you.
At those times,
allow us to be led out into the desert,
to places of simplicity and truth
where you can make us yours once again.
Amen.

Scripture: Hosea 2:14-15

Scripture Reflection

The desert is a powerful metaphor for the place where God calls us to be his own once again. This is a place where we can properly see life. Where we are blessed, and where we don't live our blessing. A place where we can be reconciled to God. What are those places in our lives where we can be reconciled to God? Those sacred places where we can see the world rightly?

Litany: Lessons from the Desert

All: Desert, teach me
The love of life.
All: Desert, teach me
The simplicity of love.
All: Desert, teach me
The beauty of simplicity.
All: Desert, teach me
The wisdom that creates beauty.
All: Desert, teach me
The insight that leads to wisdom.
All: Desert, teach me
The curiosity that leads to insight.
All: Desert, teach me
The attentiveness that leads to curiosity.
Lord, in all that I am and all that I do,
**All: Lead me out into the desert
to teach me again.**

Closing Prayer

Dear Lord,
teach us your Law of Love.
Teach us to be open
when doors close.
Teach us to be forgiving
when we are wronged.
Teach us to be understanding
when we do not know.
Teach us to be just
when persecution reigns.
Teach us to be truthful
when fear clouds our vision.
Teach us to be hopeful
when despair infects the world.
We make this prayer through
our brother Jesus, the master Teacher.
+**Amen.**

Lent I: Renewal

*I am He who blots out your transgressions
for my own sake
and I will not remember your sins.*
(Isaiah 43:25)

Preparation: *Place a glass bowl filled with sand at one side of a bare table. Around the bowl, place some small rocks of different sizes and colours. At the other end of the table, place an empty bowl. In the centre of the table, place a lit purple candle to signify God's presence in our desert. As participants enter the prayer space, have them write inside a folded slip of paper something that they would like to change in themselves this Lent, and write their name on the outside. Tell them that no one will read these. Place the slips in the empty bowl. At the end of the service, each person will take away what they hope to renew in themselves this Lent. Select readers.*

Introduction

Leader: The season of Lent is the time for renewal. We are called to renew our hearts, cleanse our souls and beg forgiveness for our sins. It is easy to spot the errors in other people's ways, yet more difficult to recognize our own failings. We need to open our hearts and minds to the cleansing element of God's Word. When we are reawakened to the glory of God's creation, we can start anew with a clean slate. Our life's burdens will seem lighter. The season of Lent offers us the wonderful chance to refresh and renew our hearts.

Invitation to Prayer

Leader: Sometimes our view of life is clouded by sin. When we accept God's forgiveness and love, our vision is cleared and we see the world more distinctly. Let us begin with the sign of the cross.

Scripture: Psalm 25:6-18

Litany: Let Us Be Renewed

There are times that we fail to do
all that we are called to do.
we lock ourselves in our private spaces
with high, thick walls.
We cannot find our way out,
for we are too busy brooding inside.
**All: Let us be renewed, O Lord.
Let us be renewed.**

At times, we see what we want
but do not really need.
We are greedy and want to own,
grasp and take whatever we see.
We falter and can become filled with evil
thoughts.
**All: Let us be renewed, O Lord.
Let us be renewed.**

We compare ourselves to others:
what they have and who they are.
We spend our time pretending and wishing.
We don't realize that we have
become envious.
**All: Let us be renewed, O Lord.
Let us be renewed.**

You teach us to love others
and to learn how to forgive.
You provide us with our life and breath,
and our wonderful world.
You have given us food to eat
and water to drink.
**All: Let us be renewed, O Lord.
Let us be renewed.**

You love us even though we're sinners;
you ask for us to follow you
and call us each by name.
You always forgive us,
no matter how many mistakes we make.
**All: Let us be renewed, O Lord.
Let us be renewed. Amen.**

Closing Prayer

God of wisdom,
help us to see ourselves honestly.
Teach us to forgive others and ourselves
for the failings to which we as humans
are prone.
We ask this through your Son, Jesus.
+**Amen.**

March

Lent II: Sacrifice

*Thus says the Lord:
I will make a way in the wilderness
and rivers in the desert.*
(Isaiah 43:14, 19)

Preparation: *Place a glass bowl filled with sand near one side of a bare table. Around the bowl, place small rocks of different sizes and colours (one for each person). At the other end of the table, place an empty bowl. At the centre of the table, place a lit a purple candle to signify God's presence in our desert. As participants enter the prayer space, have them write on a slip of paper one luxury they are sacrificing this Lent. They then fold the paper and write their name on the outside. Tell them that no one will read these. Place these slips in the empty bowl. At the end of the service, each person will take away a rock and the slip of paper on which they wrote their Lenten sacrifice. Select readers.*

Introduction

Leader: Lent is a time of sacrifice. We choose to give up something we like, as a way of remembering that Jesus gave up his life for us. Giving up and one of the luxuries of our lives during this period can make us feel as if we are living in a barren wasteland, a desert. In this arid place, it is sometimes difficult to see the oasis at the end of our journey. The season of Lent gives us the spiritual opportunity to find our way out of the desert, and to quench our thirst for the living water of Christ.

Invitation to Prayer

Leader: The wilderness can be an arid place, devoid of apparent life, colourless and barren. Let the sacrifices we make give us cleansed bodies, minds and souls, so that we can safely leave the desert and enter into our Saviour's abundance of life-giving water. Let us begin our prayer with the sign of the cross.

Scripture: Deuteronomy 8:11-20

Litany: Spiritual Wealth

Lent seems like a bleak, barren dry season, but this is the time for gaining spiritual wealth.
During these 40 days,
we are called to wait
and to endure
our small Lenten sacrifices with patience,
knowing that Jesus endured 40 days
in the desert.
All: Let our small material sacrifices turn into spiritual wealth.
We love our riches: our rich foods, our rich homes, our rich clothing, our rich lives.
We are called to share our good fortune,
to give to others and reduce our reliance
on worldly goods.
All: Let our small material sacrifices turn into spiritual wealth.

Our small sacrifices make us think about
the ultimate sacrifice that Jesus made for us.
Our patience during this season is rewarded
many times over
with the salvation Jesus gained for us.
**All: Let our small material sacrifices turn
into spiritual wealth.**
When we follow the true path
out of the desert,
we can quench our thirst
at the springs of living water.
Jesus, you are the true way.
**All: Let our small material sacrifices turn
into spiritual wealth.**

Closing Prayer

Jesus our guide,
you know that we find it difficult
to sacrifice our luxuries.
It can be as hard as the rocks
we find on the ground.
Help us to recognize
that our sacrifices during this season
bring us closer to you.
May we always remember
your great love for us.
+**Amen.**

*As participants leave, they take their slip of paper
and one rock from around the bowl of sand.*

Lent III: Resisting Temptation

*Sin is lurking at the door; its desire is for you,
but you must master it.*
(Genesis 4:7)

Preparation: *Place a glass bowl filled with sand at one side of a bare table. Around the bowl, place some small rocks of different sizes and colours. At the other end of the table, place a empty bowl. In the centre of the table, place a lit purple candle to signify God's presence in our desert. When participants enter the prayer space, have them write on slips of paper a temptation that each of them faces. They then fold the paper and write their name on the outside. Tell them that no one will read these. Place the folded slips of paper in the empty bowl. Select readers.*

Introduction

Leader: Lent is a time to resist temptation. We are reminded that Jesus, tempted in the desert by Satan, endured the pain of hunger and thirst, and resisted the seemingly easy solutions offered to him. In the desert of our lives, it is often difficult for us to resist the temptation to drink at the oasis before it is our turn. Yet the easy way out is not necessarily the right way. Lent gives us the chance to gain conviction of the true path for our lifelong faith journey.

+Scripture: Matthew 4:1-11

Invitation to Prayer

Leader: As Jesus resisted temptation in the desert, we pray to our loving God to deliver us from evil during the barren periods of our lives. Let us begin with the sign of the cross.

Litany: Deliver Us

**All: Deliver us from temptation, O Lord.
Help us to see the deep meaning of life.**
For those times when we feel
the lure and attraction of surface pleasures,
help us to avoid falling prey to their appeal.
Strengthen our weak spirits.
Help us to recognize that a silky veneer
and bright colours
can hide unsavoury ways
beneath their surfaces.
All: Deliver us from temptation, O Lord.

**All: Deliver us from evil, O Lord.
Help us to recognize sin.**
For those times when we are faced
with wickedness and iniquity,
help us to find that power within us
to turn the vice into good,
to put an end to the evil
or to turn our backs on the darkness
and face your light.
All: Deliver us from evil, O Lord.

**All: Deliver us onto the right path,
O Lord.
Help us to avoid taking the easy way out.**
For those times when we think
that the shortcut, the easy road,
the smooth way are the right paths,
help us to see that
often the road less travelled,
or the bumpy way,
and, at times, the more difficult journeys
are instead the true and just paths to you.
**All: Deliver us onto the right path,
O Lord.**

All: Deliver us to the springs of new life,
O Lord.
**Help us to make our way your way
along our faith journey to your kingdom.**
For those times when we thirst
for the living water of Christ,
help us to quench our thirst
through prayers of thanksgiving
and praise to you,
through willing service for others
and through love of our neighbour.
All: Deliver us to the springs of new life,
O Lord.

All: Deliver us from temptation.
Deliver us from evil.
Deliver us onto the right path.
Deliver us to the springs of new life.
O Lord, deliver us to you.
Amen.

Closing Prayer

God our strength,
we ask to be delivered from evil,
and pray for help in resisting temptation.
Lead us on the true path.
We ask this through Christ our Guide.
Amen.

Let us close with the words that Jesus taught us:
Our Father...+

Each person takes and then "throws away" the piece of paper on which they have written their temptation.

Lent IV: To Serve Others

*For you were called to freedom, brothers and sisters;
only do not use your freedom as an opportunity
for self-indulgence, but through love become slaves
to one another.*
(Galatians 5:13)

Preparation: *At the centre of the table, which is bare, place a lit purple candle to signify God's presence in our service to others. Select readers.*

Introduction

Leader: Lent is a time of almsgiving and prayer. We are called to give generously to those in need. We may offer our time or money, talents or joys, love or hope. We are called to be servants like Jesus. In prayer, we are asked to look at habits, attitudes and behaviours that we need to change. The season of Lent gives us the opportunity to change and grow spiritually.

Scripture: Matthew 25:34-40

Invitation to Prayer

Leader: Too often, we worry about what others think of us. We look for outside approval for our actions. Instead, let us follow the example of Jesus. +

Litany: Jesus, Teach Us to Be Faithful Servants

He wasn't a TV celebrity.
All: He was hailed by a star from the heavens.
He didn't have servants.
All: He lived to serve others.
He wasn't a millionaire.
All: He was rich in Spirit, hope and love.
He didn't drive a fancy sports car.
All: He rode a donkey or travelled on foot.
He didn't crave flowery words of flattery.
All: He craved only the plain truth.
He didn't want 5 minutes of fame and fortune.
All: He wanted a lifetime of friendship and faith.
He didn't live in a mansion.
All: He lived in the wilderness and the homes of the poor.
He didn't ask for money.
All: He asked for love, generosity and an open heart.
He didn't look for beautiful people.
All: He looked for inner beauty. The surface didn't matter.
He didn't give out autographs.
All: He gave out hope to the hopeless, love to the unloved, and miracles to believers.
Jesus, our Saviour, teach us to be
humble and faithful servants.
Guide us in our lifelong journey to you.
Help us to remain true to you
and to ourselves
and to see the inner beauty of others.
Amen.

Closing Prayer

Loving God,
we wish to be keen and devoted servants.
By your grace, help us to nurture
the lonely with our companionship,
feed the hungry and clothe the poor
with our relative richness;
and seek out and include all those
who yearn for acceptance.
We ask this through Jesus our brother.
+Amen.

Daughters of Faith (International Women's Day)

*She opens her mouth with wisdom,
and the teaching of kindness is on her tongue.*
(Proverbs 31:26)

Preparation: *Place a lit candle and pictures of women of different races, nationalities and ages on your prayer focal point. Select readers.*

Introduction

Leader: The women of our collective histories have been our mothers, our sisters, our aunts, our wives, our friends. They have nursed us, supported us, laboured with us, watched over us when we were ill, praised us when we made them proud, nurtured our imaginations, and fed our spirits. Most of all, they have loved us. We dedicate today's service to the women of our past, present and future.

Scripture: Proverbs 31:14-22

Prayer: Daughters of Faith

+As children of God, we all strive to be daughters (and sons) of faith.
Our lives are not always easy. At times, we struggle. We ask that God grant us wisdom, love, strength, hope, patience, radiance and faith as we draw ever closer to the kingdom.

All: She is wise.
Wisdom is vigilant and unfading.
She is found by those who truly seek to know her.
She guides our footsteps to God's kingdom.
**All: Hear us, O wisdom.
Grant us your grace.**

All: She is hope.
Hope is ever present
in times of expectation
as well as in times of trouble.
She generously gives us
the will to stay on the path
wherever our life's journey takes us.
She gives us the determination to go on.
**All: Hear us, O hope.
Grant us your grace.**

All: She is strength.
Strength is the intense inner power
to do God's will
even in the face of difficulty.
She is passionate, dedicated and fervent
in her desire to know God.
**All: Hear us, O strength.
Grant us your grace.**

All: She is radiance.
Radiance is breathtaking, ageless beauty
that cannot be viewed on the surface,
but resides within her spirit
and is rooted in her soul.
Her radiance shines ever brightly
for those who know how to see.
**All: Hear us, O radiance.
Grant us your grace.**

All: She is patience.
Patience is the calm awareness
that tells her that true worth
is not measured by minutes and hours.
She willingly embraces the vast difference
between our perception of time and God's,
knowing that when we wait patiently,

what we attain with God's grace
will be truly worthwhile.
**All: Hear us, O patience.
Grant us your grace.**

All: She is love.
Love is unending, eternal
and all encompassing.
She does not ask what you do
but only what you are.
**All: Hear us, O love.
Grant us your grace.**

All: She is faith.
Faith is unspoken trust.
She is unbreakable, unshakeable knowledge
in our true God-given potential.
**All: Hear us, O faith.
Grant us your grace.**

All: She is woman,
and without God, she cannot be.
Truly wise.
Ever hopeful.
Firmly strong.
Always radiant.
Endlessly patient.
Eternally loving.
Forever faithful.
**All: Hear us, O God, hear our prayer.
Grant us your grace.
Amen.**

Reflection

Leader: As the women in Scripture knew, being a daughter of faith, a child of God, and a follower of truth meant being steadfast: committed to their goals. It also meant being both flexible and determined. Their paths were not predictable. Like us, these women had the usual human foibles and faults. Each woman had her own story and her own motivation. Yet, despite their uniqueness, they shared many traits. All wanted the best for their people, whether their immediate families or their communities. All were willing to sacrifice to attain their goals. Most importantly, all had utter faith and belief in God's power to influence their lives.

The closing prayer is for these women of our past, as well as those of our present and our future.

Closing Prayer

**All: They were women and daughters
of faith,
loving people of every race.
They were leaders who were patient
and strong.
We all belong to their families.**
Eve, Sarah and Holy Mary
were mothers, blessed and true.
Abigail and Esther were wives of kings.
Hear the message of their stories.

Rachel, Leah, Ruth and Martha
were devoted, and followed truth.
Judith and Deborah saved their people.
Miriam was a leader of faith.
**All: For they were women
and daughters of faith,
loving people of every race.
They were leaders who taught us love.
They were truly blessed by God.**

Maya Angelou, Mother Teresa
and Dorothy Day,
poets, saints, advocates and writers,
mothers, cousins, aunts, sisters, friends:
the circle of faith continually grows.

**All: For we are women and daughters of faith,
loving people of every race.
We are leaders. We instill love.
We are truly blessed by God.
+Amen.**

Answer the Call to Persevere

The one who endures to the end will be saved.
(Mark 13:13)

Preparation: Place a lit candle and a Bible on the prayer table. To represent perseverance, arrange items (such as test papers, pens, textbooks and other items that signify chores and jobs that participants are required to do) around the candle without hiding it. Select readers.

Opening Prayer

+ God of our beginning and end,
God, the Alpha and Omega,
your love for us is everlasting,
your wisdom boundless,
your mercy endless.
Teach us to persevere in prayer,
that we might one day rejoice with you
in heaven
and live in your Divine Presence for evermore.
We ask this through your Son, Jesus Christ.
Amen.

Scripture: Luke 11:5-13

Litany: Perseverance

Leader: We will continue to pray
for the less fortunate.
**All: Eternal God,
we answer your call to persevere.**
We will remain vigilant
and will act for those who need our aid.
**All: Eternal God,
we answer your call to persevere.**
We will continue our efforts
to free the oppressed.
**All: Eternal God,
we answer your call to persevere.**
We will be ever watchful
for the ordinary miracles
you show us every day.
**All: Eternal God,
we answer your call to persevere.**
We will love and respect
all of God's children,
regardless of race or creed.
**All: Eternal God,
we answer your call to persevere.**
We will remain constant
in our praise of your Son, our Saviour.
**All: Eternal God,
we answer your call to persevere.**
We will be ever thankful to the Holy Spirit
for the gifts we have received.
**All: Eternal God,
we answer your call to persevere.**
We will strive to follow your Word
in every deed and thought.
**All: Eternal God,
we answer your call to persevere.**
We will remain steadfast in our hope
for everlasting life with you.
Amen.

Let us now pray to God with the words
that Jesus taught us.
Our Father …

Closing Prayer

God of all that is good,
in our prayers
we worship you with reverence,
we praise you with love,
we thank you with humility.
May we persevere in our daily prayers to you.
+Amen.

March Break Blessing

By God's will I may come to you with joy and be refreshed.
(Romans 15:32)

Preparation: *Place a purple cloth on the prayer focal point. Select readers.*

Opening Prayer

+Loving God,
we will soon leave for our March Break.
Accept our weariness and fatigue as signs of our devotion to your beloved children.
May our travel or rest be a time of renewal and refreshment.
Amen.

Scriptural Reflection on the Journey

Reader 1: God calls Abraham to settle in Canaan.
Reader 2: But I will be a stranger in a strange land.
Reader 3: "Go and know that I am God."

Reader 1: God brings the Israelites out of Egypt.
Reader 2: But in the freedom of the desert we longed for the security of Egypt.
Reader 3: "I will be your God and you will be my people".

Reader 1: Once again, the Jewish people are exiled, this time in Babylon.
Reader 2: By the waters of Babylon we sat down and wept.
Reader 3: "Comfort my people."
Reader 1: The apostles journey to the ends of the earth, spreading the Gospel,
Reader 2: Sometimes to praise, sometimes to martyrdom.
Reader 3: "I will be with you always."

Leader: God of the journey,
we walk, pray and celebrate with you.

Reflection

In our hearts
let us create a sanctuary,
a sacred place
where we can hear the voice
of the Holy One of God say to us:
"Be not afraid, you are my beloved,
I have carved your name on the palm of my hand."

You are blessed so that you bless;
you are graced so that you become grace;
you are enlightened so that you can enlighten;
you are loved so that you can love;
you have been taught so that you can now teach God's Word.

Prayer of Gratitude

Loving God,
it is good to be here,
on the verge of vacation.
May our gratitude for this moment
extend back through time,
tracing the ways
you have taught us wisdom,
and extend into the future with hope.
We make this prayer in the name of Jesus,
the wandering preacher.
+**Amen.**

God of the Journey (St. Patrick's Day)

*From his fullness we have all received,
grace upon grace.*
(John 1:16)

Preparation: *On the prayer focal point, place a purple cloth to represent Lent. On top, place shamrocks or other small, green objects to represent St. Patrick. Other symbols of the day may be added. Select readers.*

Opening Prayer

+God of the journey,
you invited Patrick to walk with you
in a land far from home:
spreading your word,
teaching your truth,
describing your beauty.
May we learn from Patrick
the courage to say "yes,"
the courage to walk along difficult paths,
the courage to be true to you.
Amen.

Scripture: Matthew 28:16-20

Scripture Reflection

Patrick, our brother,
you took this Gospel to heart.
You became its message.
You lived its truth through deed and word.

Patrick,
you blessed the Irish soul
with your compassion and imagination,
with your conviction and perseverance.
You bless all our souls
with your joy and reverence.
For these gifts we give thanks.

Prayer in the Style of St. Patrick

Reader 1: We join here with those before us
in our circle of loving.
We recognize
the love of God, three in one,
the guidance of Mary and all the saints,
the dearly departed,
the children who are yet to be born,
and those with us today
in this sacred place and in this sacred time.

Reader 2: Grace flow through us.
Grace flow above us.
Grace flow below us.
Grace flow between us.
Grace flow around us.
Grace flow towards us.
Grace flow from us.

Reader 3: May the whisper of the sacred be
yours in trying times,
to strengthen you,
to encourage you.
May the touch of the holy
be yours in joyful times,
to humble you with gratitude,
to dance and laugh your love.
May the caress of the Spirit
be yours in your losses,
to hold you and to heal you.
Amen.

Closing Prayer

May your joy linger.
May your hope direct you.
May your patience protect you.
May your gratitude be deepened.
May your beauty increase.
We make this prayer in the name of Jesus,
beloved centre of St. Patrick's life.
+Amen.

You Called Mary (Annunciation)

Greetings, favoured one!
(Luke 1:28)

Preparation: *On the focal point for prayer, place a purple cloth for Lent or a white cloth for Easter. On the cloth, place a Bible and symbols of Our Lady, such as a statuette, rosary, icon or flower. Select readers.*

Opening Prayer

+God of the Annunciation,
God of surprises,
send angels of inspiration
to startle us,
to bring fresh life,
to reawaken our sense of justice.
Help us to taste
not only the sweetness of life …
and give you thanks,
but also the bitterness of injustice …
and work to remove it.
Awaken us again to our true calling,
our true mission:
to walk with you in the paths laid out for us.
Amen.

Scripture: Luke 1:26-35

Reflection: Mary's Call

Gracious God, you called Mary
**All: To give birth to your Son,
to give birth to goodness,
to give birth to light.**
For nine months,
Mary felt love growing within.
You call us also
**All: To carry your love,
to bring your truth and justice
into the world,
to be a sign of hope and peace.**

Litany: Annunciations

Leader: Angels such as Gabriel
spread news of God's goodness
to the world.
Let us give thanks to those other angels
who remind us of God's love:

For the returning robin,
singing in the spring,
All: We give thanks.
For buds swelling on trees,
All: We give thanks.
For white clouds dancing across blue skies,
All: We give thanks.
For cracks in the ice and for melting snow,
All: We give thanks.

Closing Prayer

Master Teacher,
Interrupt our complacency
All: with greetings.
Interrupt our fears
All: with encouragement.
Interrupt our reluctance
All: with determination.
May we see the Gabriels among us
All: instructing and commissioning us
to live in your justice,
to be servants of your peace,
to be bearers of your hope.
We make this prayer
in the name of Mary's Son, Jesus.
+Amen.

April

Into Jerusalem (Beginning Holy Week)

*Hosanna! Blessed is the one
who comes in the name of the Lord!*
(John 12:13)

Preparation: *On the prayer focal point, place a purple cloth. Place on it a Bible, candle and symbols of Holy Week: palms, cross, bread and wine. Select readers. If you are not going to use the Holy Thursday service, you may want to incorporate the ritual of the washing of the feet or hands in today's service (see "The Upper Room").*

Opening Prayer

+God of love,
from Palm Sunday to Good Friday,
we follow the last few days of Jesus,
your Son, in Jerusalem:
a journey towards death,
a journey towards eternal life,
a journey of love.
His journey is also our journey.
God of love,
may we look with eyes of compassion
on this journey
and see our own joys and losses
in the journey of Jesus.
Amen.

The Entry into Jerusalem

Reader 1: I am Jerusalem,
I am the City of David,
the City of Longing,
awaiting the time,
preparing,
hoping.
Are you the one?
Are you the one on the colt
coming down through the olive groves?
Are you the Prince of Jerusalem?
The Prince of Peace?
Are you coming to set us free?

Reader 2: I sit waiting,
thinking I'm ready,
preparing for you.

Reader 3: When Jesus had come near Bethphage and Bethany,
at the place called the Mount of Olives,
he sent two of the disciples, saying,
"Go into the village ahead of you,
and as you enter it you will find tied there
a colt that has never been ridden.
Untie it, and bring it here.
If anyone asks you, 'Why are you untying it?' just say this: 'The Lord needs it.'"
(see Mark 11:1-3)

Reader 4: But am I ready?
Ready to carry you into the city?
To dwell in the Jerusalem of my heart?

Reader 5: So those who were sent departed
and found it as he had told them.
As they were untying the colt,
its owners asked them,
"Why are you untying that colt?"
They said, "The Lord needs it."
Then they brought it to Jesus;
and after throwing their cloaks on the colt,
they set Jesus on it.
As he rode along, people kept spreading
their cloaks on the road.
(see Mark 11:4-8)

Reader 1: Will my words be honest?
Will my deeds be loving?
Will my heart be hopeful?

Reader 2: As he was now approaching
the path down from the Mount of Olives,
the whole multitude of the disciples
began to praise God joyfully with a loud voice
for all the deeds of power
that they had seen, saying,

All: "Blessed is the one who comes in the name of the Lord! Hosanna in the highest heaven!" *(Mark 11:9-10)*

Litany: Entering Jerusalem

As Jesus rode in triumph into Jerusalem,
All: May we be blessed by our families and friends.
As Jesus taught the crowds in the city,
All: May we teach the law of love with our words and example.
As Jesus stood up to the desecrators of the Temple,
All: May we have the courage to stand up for what is right in our community.
As Jesus gathered the disciples,
All: May we cherish and honour our friends.
As Jesus washed the feet of his disciples,
All: May we never be too proud to serve those in need.
As Jesus ate and drank the meal of remembrance,
All: May we continue this Eucharist in ritual and deed.
As Jesus prayed for strength in Gethsemane,
All: May we pray for courage to face our trials.
As Jesus was calm in the face of his persecutors,
All: May we face our testing with equanimity and peace.
As Jesus faced his death,
All: May we face our death in the peace of coming home.
Amen.

Closing Reflection

Love came among us.
Some listened. Some were scornful.
Truth came to teach us.
Some learned. Some closed their hearts.
Justice came to live here.
Some welcomed. Some rejected.
Look at ourselves today.
Do we see Jesus in love, truth and justice?
Do we show scorn, close our hearts
and reject?
Or do we listen, learn and welcome
in the name of Jesus?

Closing Prayer

Loving God,
bless our steps towards Easter.
Let our words, our silence, and our deeds
echo your love for us.
Bring comfort and peace in our anxiety.
Bring wisdom and integrity
into our daily lives.
May we always feel your Spirit within
and around us.
We make this prayer in the name of the one
who was crucified for us.
+Amen.

Ritual

Leader: Let us conclude with a sign of peace.

All exchange a sign of peace.

Help Us to Love (Stations of the Cross)

Jesus committed no sin, and no deceit was found in his mouth. When he was abused, he did not return abuse. When he suffered, he did not threaten; but he entrusted himself to the one who judges justly.
(1 Peter 2:22-23)

Preparation: *You will need enough space for everyone to move freely around the room. Place 14 candles around the room to signify the 14 Stations. As the group reaches each station, light the candle there. At the end of the service, when all candles are lit, participants form a circle around the room. Select readers.*

Opening Prayer

+Loving God,
as we speak our words for the journey,
let us open our hearts to receive
the generous gift of love that Christ offers us.
Despite our weaknesses,
despite our sins,
despite our failings,
Jesus cherishes each of us.
When we truly receive him,
we are cleansed.
Jesus is our loving example.
As we walk the Stations of the Cross,
teach us to keep our hearts ever open to
your blessing.
Help us to love.
We ask this through your Son,
Jesus Christ our Lord.
Amen.

Scripture: Acts 8:32-33

Leader: The First Station:
Jesus is condemned by Pontius Pilate
Reader 1: Though you did nothing wrong,
you have been condemned to die.
Yet you do not complain.
You do not condemn those
who condemn you.
You are still filled with love.
**All: Help us, Jesus, to always love,
even in the face of hatred.
Let us follow in the way of the Lord.**

Leader: The Second Station:
Jesus takes up the cross
Reader 2: You are made to carry
your heavy cross.
Yet you make no objection or protest
about the burden placed upon you.
The cross cuts into your flesh.
Yet, you are still filled with love.
**All: Help us, Jesus, to always love,
even in the face of physical pain.
Let us follow in the way of the Lord.**

Leader: The Third Station:
Jesus falls for the first time
Reader 1: The weight of the cross
taxes your body.
You fall under its heavy weight.
Yet, you are still filled with love,
**All: Help us, Jesus, to always love,
even when we fall.
Let us follow in the way of the Lord.**

Leader: The Fourth Station:
Jesus meets his mother
Reader 2: You meet your grieving mother.
She weeps to see your suffering.
You comfort her despite your pain.
You are filled with love.
**All: Help us, Jesus, to always love,
even when we see pain reflected
in the eyes of our loved ones.
Let us follow in the way of the Lord.**

Leader: The Fifth Station:
Simon of Cyrene carries the cross
Reader 1: Simon helps you.
He bears the weight of the heavy cross
for a while.
You did not ask for his help,
but you are grateful to him just the same.
You are filled with love.
**All: Help us, Jesus, to always love,
even when we need help
from those around us.
Let us follow in the way of the Lord.**

Leader: The Sixth Station:
Veronica wipes the face of Jesus
Reader 2: The strain of bearing the cross
makes you sweat.
Veronica's gift is to wipe your face
and cool your brow.
You are filled with love.
**All: Help us, Jesus, to always love when
we accept gifts from others.
Let us follow in the way of the Lord.**

Leader: The Seventh Station:
Jesus falls the second time
Reader 1: The weight of the cross
becomes almost too much to bear.
You fall a second time.
You get but a few moments' respite
from the heavy burden.
Yet you are filled with love.
**All: Help us, Jesus, to always love,
even when we think it is too hard
to get up after we have fallen.
Let us follow in the way of the Lord.**

Leader: The Eighth Station:
Jesus meets the women of Jerusalem
Reader 2: The women of Jerusalem weep
for you, yet you pray for them and tell them
not to weep for you but for their children.
You are filled with love.
**All: Help us, Jesus, to always love,
even when we need to support others.
Let us follow in the way of the Lord.**

Leader: The Ninth Station:
Jesus falls the third time
Reader 1: The crushing weight of the cross
causes you to fall a third time.
It is even more difficult to rise now.
The cross continues to cut into your flesh.
Yet you are filled with love.
**All: Help us, Jesus, to always love,
even when we believe
that we cannot get up again.
Let us follow in the way of the Lord.**

Leader: The Tenth Station:
Jesus is stripped of his garments
Reader 2: Your captors strip you
and cast lots for your clothing.
Yet you are filled with love.
**All: Help us, Jesus, to always love,
even if others try to take away our dignity.
Let us follow in the way of the Lord.**

Leader: The Eleventh Station:
Jesus is nailed to the Cross
Reader 1: The soldiers brutally nail
your wrists and feet to the cross.
The searing pain is agonizing.
They have no regard for your suffering.
They laugh at you.
Yet, you are still filled with love.
**All: Help us, Jesus, to always love,
even in the face of persecution.
Let us follow in the way of the Lord.**

Leader: The Twelfth Station: Jesus dies
Reader 2: You die on the cross.
Yet you do not blame those
who have crucified you.
You are still filled with love.
**All: Help us, Jesus, to always love,
even in the face of death.
Let us follow in the way of the Lord.**

Leader: The Thirteenth Station:
The body of Jesus is removed from the cross
Reader 1: Your sacred body is removed
from the cross
as your mother and others look on.
Those who killed you
do not know what they have done.
You still love.
**All: Help us, Jesus, to always love,
even when we feel that we have lost
our battles.
Let us follow in the way of the Lord.**

Leader: The Fourteenth Station:
Jesus is laid in the tomb
Reader 2: Your body is prepared
and then laid to rest in a tomb.
A large stone is rolled in front
of the entrance to keep your body safe.
**All: Help us, Jesus, to always love,
even when it seems like the end is at hand.
Let us follow in the way of the Lord.**

Closing Reflection:

Leader: We have walked the way
of the Lord
and are now surrounded by a circle
of his light.
Let us remember that just as this circle
is continuous,
with no beginning or end,
so, too, is the love of Christ.
Do not break the cycle of love.
These words for the journey
will bring us closer to God.
We will grow as we journey
in faith together. +

The Upper Room (Holy Thursday)

He will show you a large room upstairs.
(Mark 14:15)

Preparations: *On the prayer focal point, place a purple cloth, Bible, candle, bowl of water and a towel. Bread and wine may also be placed there. Select readers.*

Opening Prayer

+Jesus, our brother,
washer of feet,
teacher of wisdom,
you are the reason that we gather
to remember that last meal in Jerusalem.
You graced that feast with deep meaning.
Touch our hearts with
a commitment to that memory,
a commitment to serve and to love.
Amen.

Ritual

The leader carries the bowl of water to each participant and washes their hands or feet. As they are being washed, participants think of a person who has been an important servant leader for them. They say, "I am washed with the memory of [name of person], a reflection of the love of Jesus Christ."

Scripture: Matthew 26:26-29

Scripture Reflection

On this day,
Jesus celebrated the Last Supper
with his disciples.
They gathered in the upper room.
Jesus washed their feet,
broke the bread and shared the wine.
He said, "Do this in memory of me."
They were gathered in the upper room
so Jesus could tell them
that they were loved,
that he came to serve,
that they must do the same,
that he would soon be leaving them,
that, even so,
the Spirit would always be with them.

Litany: The Upper Room

Let us celebrate the gifts of Holy Thursday:
For the wisdom of Jesus,
All: We give thanks.
For the hospitality of the table,
All: We give thanks.
For the commission to servant leadership,
All: We give thanks.
For the sacred bread of life,
All: We give thanks.
For the holy wine that flows through time,
All: We give thanks.

Closing Prayer

Dear Jesus,
at the Last Supper, you blessed us
with the beauty of the Eucharist,
a sign of love and unity.
Your song at this meal
resonates through our liturgy and our lives.
It echoes in our work and our play.
Your song calls us forward
along paths of goodness and justice,
along paths that will lead us home.
+**Amen.**

Easter Light

I pray that the God of our Lord Jesus Christ, the Father of glory, may give you a spirit of wisdom and revelation as you come to know him, so that, with the eyes of your heart enlightened, you may know what is the hope to which he has called you.
(Ephesians 1:17-18)

Preparation: *Place lit candles around the room to represent God's presence all around us. Place a lit Paschal candle on the prayer table. As participants enter, give each one a taper. During the Litany, they will light their tapers from the Paschal candle. Select readers.*

Introduction

Leader: At Easter, we celebrate the Risen Lord, who was dead and was laid in a cold, dark cave, but who is now resurrected to new life, new warmth and new light. We rejoice in his light of new life.

Opening Prayer

+Jesus our Saviour,
your light sustains us in times of darkness.
Jesus our guide,
your light illuminates the right path for us.
Jesus our strength,
your light helps us to push away
the shadows of the night.
Let us open the eyes of our minds
and hearts to listen to the Word of Light,
the Word of God.
We ask this through your Son,
our Risen Lord.
Amen.

Scripture: 1 John 1:5-7, 2:9-11

Litany: May We Live in the Light of the Lord

During the Litany, all approach the Paschal candle and light their tapers.

Leader: The light of Christ shines
all over the world,
through all his creations, great and small.
Jesus has opened the doors
from the *darkness* of sin
to the *light* of heaven,
from the *darkness* of death
to the *light* of new life,
from the *darkness* of war
to the *light* of his peace.
May we ever live in the light of Christ.
All: May we live in the light of the Lord.
Loving God,
creator of all in the universe,
we thank you for calling us
to be members of your holy people.
We thank you for inviting us
through the doorway
into your heavenly kingdom, and we say:
All: May we live in the light of the Lord.
Lord Jesus Christ,
we thank you for forgiving us our sins
and for sharing with us your risen life
through your great sacrifice.
We thank you for the new life
you promise us, and we say:
All: May we live in the light of the Lord.
Holy Spirit of God,
we thank you for healing our broken hearts
and judgmental souls.

We thank you for filling us with your love
and guiding us in the way of peace,
and we say:
All: May we live in the light of the Lord.
Let us remember that the God of light,
who set us free,
dwells with us now and always.
Alleluia! Alleluia! May we live in your light!
All: Alleluia! Alleluia!
May we live in the light of the Lord.
Amen.

Closing Prayer

God of love,
we thank you for your Son,
the true light of the world.
May he reveal to us the way to you,
and may we always look to his light
to guide us in our lives here on earth
and on our journey to you in heaven.

Let us always remember that,
as faithful followers of Jesus,
we carry his light within our minds,
within our hearts,
and within our souls.
Let us learn to allow that light
to shine through us every day.
Let us now go in peace and light,
to love and serve you, our Lord.
Amen.

May I carry the light of the Lord
within my mind, heart and soul.

Leader extinguishes taper.

All: May we carry the light of the Lord
within our minds, hearts and souls.

All extinguish tapers.

+Amen.

Easter Blessing

He has been raised.
(Mark 16:6)

Preparation: *On your prayer focal point, place a white cloth, Paschal candle, Bible, and symbols of Easter, such as a lily, an egg, or a picture of a sunrise. Select readers.*

Opening Prayer

+God of Easter morning,
fill us with hope and joy.
Give us voices to sing our Alleluias
with the heavenly choir.
Let our voices resonate with the beauty
of that first Easter dawn.
May that spirit of joy flow through all we do
in the fields of your love.
Amen.

Scripture: Matthew 28:1-10

Litany: Easter Morning

Reader 1: Early, very early,
when darkness faded, faded, faded
in the morning's first light,
first light shone so bright,
shone so bright on those women.

Reader 2: But the tomb was empty:
empty of understanding,
empty of expectation,
empty of reason,
in that place.

Reader 1: Where despair turned to hope,
Reader 2: Where hope turned to wonder,
Reader 1: Where wonder turned to awe,
Reader 2: Where awe turned to joy,
Reader 1: Where joy turned faith,
Reader 2: Where faith turned to love.

Reader 1: The women spoke:
Reader 2: And love will pour forth,
Readers 2, 3: And love will spread
like perfume,
Readers 2, 3, 4: And love will pass from
heart to heart,
Readers 2, 3, 4, 5: And love will take root
in the soils of justice,
Readers 2, 3, 4, 5, 6: And love will put
blossoms on the tree of crucifixion.

Reader 1: And that tree of wisdom
will teach us to walk in paths of wisdom,
truth and beauty.
Reader 3: Yes, we will stumble,
Reader 4: Yes, we will fall,
Reader 5: Yes, we will be broken,
Reader 6: Yes, we will walk on.

Reader 1: On that morning, that bright,
bright morning.
Reader 2: On this morning, this bright,
bright morning.

Closing Prayer

God of hope,
resurrected Christ,
Spirit of new beginnings,
May we be blessed by the touch of spring:
rain falling from the heavens,
washing us clean,
telling us that life is sacred.

May we be blessed by the sight of spring:
flowers breaking through winter's crust,
telling us that life is beautiful.

May we be blessed by the sound of children
playing in the garden,
shouting with happiness,
telling us that life is joyful.

May we blessed by the taste of Easter eggs,
hidden and then found,
telling us that life is sweet.

May we blessed by the smell of
Easter bread baking in the oven,
awakening our senses,
telling us that life is good.

May we be blessed by memory
this Easter time:
of loved ones,
of loved places,
telling us that your love is always here.
We make this prayer in the name of Jesus.
+**Amen.**

Our Greatest Gift (Reverence)

And they shall stand every morning, thanking and praising the Lord, and likewise at evening.
(1 Chronicles 23:30)

Preparation: *Place a lit candle and a Bible on the prayer table. Select readers.*

Invitation to Prayer

Leader: Every living being that has breath owes its very life to God's grace.
Happy are those who are blessed by our God.
Happy are those who trust in the Lord's unending love for us.
With awe and reverence,
let us now join in praising God
the Creator of all life
as we listen to the Word.

+**Scripture**: Revelation 15:3-4

Reverence Prayer

All: Our faith gives us hope
for everlasting life.
Our worship reveals to us sacredness.
Our love brings us light
in times of darkness.
Leader: But our reverence allows us
to celebrate the delight
of being cherished children of God.

All: Our compassion leads us
to understanding.
Our trust brings us your healing.
Our sincerity brings us forgiveness.
Leader: But our reverence allows us
to honour God's gracious gift of life.

All: Our joy gives us freedom.
Our differences make us grow.
Our respect teaches us acceptance.
Leader: But our reverence allows us
to fully appreciate the relevance
of the Word of God.

All: Our thankfulness is for your blessings.
Our praise is for your holy name.
Our devotion is for the Trinity.
Leader: But our reverence is our gift to you.
Our reverence is forever yours.
Amen.

Closing Prayer/Ritual

Leader: Please extend your hands and confer the following blessing on each other:

All: May you walk in wonder.
May you be filled with awe.
May you be imbued with the Spirit.
And may your reverence for God be endless,
For in living in reverence of our God, you will be ever blessed.
+Amen.

Speak to the Earth (Earth Week)

And God saw that it was good.
(Genesis 1:10)

Preparations: *Place a green cloth on the table; you may want to overlay it partially with white if it is Easter season. On the cloth, place a candle, Bible and natural objects such as flowers, pine cones, seashells, water. Select readers.*

Introduction

Leader: We celebrate Earth Week
in our prayers today.
Not to ask for hands to clean up
the environmental mess we are in,
for God has already given us those,
but for the wisdom to let nature
be our teacher
and for the courage to do the right thing.

+Scripture: Job 12:7-9 (adapted)

Reader 1: A reading from the Book of Job.
Now ask the beasts and they will teach you,
Reader 2: Ask the birds of the air
and they will teach you.
Reader 1: Or speak to the earth
and it will teach you,
Reader 2: And the fish of the sea
and they will teach you,
Readers 1, 2: Of the glory of God.

Scripture Reflection

Reader 1: Let us be wise students
of the earth,
so that we can learn strength
from the storm,
Reader 2: Patience from the pines,
Reader 1: Warmth from the sun,
Reader 2: Joy from a mountain stream,
Reader 1: Peacefulness from ocean waves,
Reader 2: And hope from a spring
wildflower.
Reader 1. God of creation,
may we have the wisdom to treat
your creation with deep reverence.

Creation Prayer

God of creation,
open our eyes,
open our ears
to the lesson of creation
so that we may learn:
the joy of daffodils dancing in the April sun;
the strength of a blade of grass
pushing through asphalt;
the stillness of a mountain lake
reflecting a full moon;
the insistence of young robins
yearning to live;
the persistence of waves
washing against a stony beach;
the grace of a hawk wheeling on an updraft;
the balance of growing shoots
and falling leaves;
the peace of soft rain on lilacs.
God grant us the wisdom of forest and field.
Amen.

Ritual

Pass a tray containing different elements or photographs of the natural world.

Leader: Each rock or leaf or twig has something to teach of us if we open our imagination. In quiet contemplation, let us reflect on the lesson nature teaches us.

Litany: The Garden

God of gardens, God of children,
in your garden,
you ask us to care for growing seeds.
All: May we serve with love.
In your garden,
you ask us to cultivate the soil.
All: May we serve with justice.
In your garden,
you ask us to admire its beauty.
All: May we serve in awe.
Amen.

Closing Prayer

Dear God,
through your wonderful works of creation,
you teach us the simple truths we need
to be happy
if we have the ears to hear
and the eyes to see.
In the beauty of creation,
may we see that your love for the world
is ever bright.
May we take time to give thanks
to you, God,
for the majesty of your world.
We make this prayer in the name of Jesus.
+**Amen.**

Servants of Love (Administrative Professionals' Day)

Everyone who loves is born of God and knows God.
(1 John 4:7)

Preparations: *Place a cloth on the table. On the cloth place a candle, Bible and flowers or other decorations. Select readers.*

Opening Prayer

God of love,
we give thanks for these wonderful people
who support Catholic education.
May they continue to be treasured
by the students and staff of this school.
Amen.

Scripture: Matthew 9:35-38

Scripture Reflection

Jesus taught us that we are a community
and we need each other to live.
God taught us to live in gratitude.
Today we give our thanks
to these administrative professionals
who do so much for the students we serve.
They are a vital part of the community
of love that supports Catholic education.
For them, we give thanks.
Amen.

Ritual

All stand facing the administrative professionals with arms outstretched in blessing during the litany.

Litany: Blessing of Administrative Professionals

For their caring and dedication,
All: May they be blessed.
For their patience and kindness,
All: May they be blessed.
For their intelligence and skill,
All: May they be blessed.
For their warmth and friendship,
All: May they be blessed.
Loving God,
hold our friends close to your heart
now and always.
Amen.

Administrative professionals say:

AP: God of caring,
take our hands and let them
All: Craft your work.
AP: Take our feet and let them
All: Walk in your ways.
AP: Take our ears and let them
All: Hear your Word.
AP: Take our eyes and let them
All: See your world.
AP: Take our minds and let them
All: Act with your wisdom.
AP: Take our hearts and let them see
with your passion.
All: Amen.

Closing Prayer

God of compassion,
bless your servants of love gathered here,
especially the administrative professionals.
May they be instruments of your love
in all they do.
Through their gifts of organization
and communication,
they help to build your kingdom.
Guide them and protect them.
May they always live in your love.
+Amen.

May

Model of Love (St. Joseph the Worker)

The Child continued to grow and become strong.
(Luke 2:40)

Preparation: *On the prayer focal point, place a cloth in the appropriate liturgical colour. Place on it a Bible, a lit candle and a picture of St. Joseph or the Holy Family. Select readers.*

Introduction

Leader: The Feast of St. Joseph the Worker is celebrated on May 1, International Labour Day. St. Joseph, the earthly father of Jesus, is Canada's patron saint. Today's prayer service remembers St. Joseph in his roles as guardian and model.

+**Scripture:** Luke 2:51-52

Scripture Reflection

Dear St. Joseph,
you were a parent.
You know about the hard work
of raising a child in uncertain times.
Pray with us to Jesus, that
when there is suffering,
we may model resilience;
when there is despair,
we may model hope;
when there is fear,
we may model love;
when there is harshness,
we may model gentleness.

As parents embrace their children,
may we also be embraced by your love.
Amen.

Litany: St. Joseph, Worker and Parent

St. Joseph, we thank you for your care
and loving concern for workers everywhere.
As patron saint of Canada, pray with us
that all workers might understand
the dignity and importance of work
in creating a Civilization of Love.

For all those who are forced to leave
their land for the sake of freedom,
All: St. Joseph, pray for us.
For all parents who are raising children
in harsh circumstances,
All: St. Joseph, pray for us.
For all who are unemployed
or underemployed,
All: St. Joseph, pray for us.
For the gift of your work and love,
All: We give thanks.
Amen.

Closing Prayer

Let us serve generously
and walk with St. Joseph the Worker by
feeding the hungry,
befriending the lonely,
comforting the hurting,
affirming the afflicted,
encouraging the despairing, and
helping the overworked.
We make this prayer in the name of Jesus.
+**Amen.**

Created in Your Image (Catholic Education Week)

God created humankind in his image.
(Genesis 1:27)

Preparation: *In the prayer focal point, place a candle, a Bible, a cloth reflecting the colour of the liturgical season, and pictures of people who reveal the diversity of those mentioned in the litany. Select readers.*

Opening Prayer

+Creator God,
you have blessed us with goodness and love.
We give thanks for being called to serve
as educators;
we give thanks for the students in our care;
we give thanks for those who created
our Catholic schools.
May our work today be a worthy echo
of your grace,
and may our celebrations be touched
by your joy.
Amen.

Scripture: Genesis 1:26-31

Scripture Reflection

Leader: Our original blessing
is that we are created and cherished by God.
In a world marred by ugliness and despair,
it is easy to be formed by the negative.
Let our reflection today be a reminder
that we are a blessing; we are sacred.

Litany: The Image of God

We gather, the oldest and the youngest,
All: Created in the image of God.
The hurting and the healing,
All: Created in the image of God.
The despairing and the hopeful,
All: Created in the image of God.
The leader and the learner,
All: Created in the image of God.
The server and the served,
All: Created in the image of God.
Those who care and the cared for,
All: Created in the image of God.
Amen.

Ritual

As a sign of mutual reverence, each person traces the sign of the cross over the hands or forehead of a neighbour while saying, "You are an image of God."

Closing Prayer

Christ of the journey,
may we remember
that you are always walking with us.
You are always by our side
as we create schools marked by
joy and justice,
compassion and community,
truth and wisdom,
peace and reverence.
When we lose our way,
bring us back to the path.
Remind us that we are blessed,
that we are sacred,
and that we are called to reflect your grace.
May you continue to bless those
who work in Catholic schools.
We make this prayer in the name
of Jesus the teacher.
+Amen.

On Being a Caring Family Member

I have no greater joy than this, to hear that my children are walking in the truth.
(3 John 1:4)

Preparation: *On the prayer centre table, place a cloth of the appropriate colour for the liturgical season. Also place a candle for each person, a Bible and a crucifix there. Select readers.*

Invitation to Prayer

The ancient Chinese philosopher Confucius wrote,
"To put the world right in order,
we must first put the nation in order;
to put the nation in order,
we must first put the family in order;
to put the family in order,
we must first cultivate our personal life;
we must first set our hearts right."

We have a responsibility
to set our hearts right …
but what does that mean?
It means praying, forgiving,
peacemaking, loving.

Opening Prayer

+Loving God,
bless us gathered here today
and bless our families.
May they be models for our society:
little communities of refuge and hope,
little communities of understanding
and wisdom,
little communities of prayer and play.
And may we continue to draw ever closer
to your law of love.
Amen.

Ritual

Each person is invited to light a candle, to represent their family. As they light their candle, participants name their family members aloud.

Scripture: Luke 2:41-52

Scripture Reflection

Jesus,
you call us to live as caring family members,
yet you knew what it was like to have family
that was stressed:
yours was a refugee family in Egypt;
you went missing because of a breakdown
in communication;
you were misunderstood by your parents
in the Temple.
Yet you were taught by your earthly
and heavenly families.
You grew in wisdom and knowledge.
Let us treasure, as Mary did,
your growth in love, compassion and justice.
Help us grow beyond our family difficulties
to become little communities of witness
and hope.

Litany: For Families

Gracious God,
continue to help our families grow in love
and wisdom.
In times of turmoil,
All: Bring peace and understanding.
When words wound,
All: Bring compassion and hope.
When sickness and injury touch us,
All: Bring patience and healing.

In times of loss and grief,
All: Bring comfort and strength.
In times of joy,
All: Bring celebration and thanksgiving.
When fear threatens,
All: Bring love and trust.
When we weary from work,
All: Bring relaxation and reflection.
In times of haste,
All: Bring us the slow wisdom of grace.
Amen.

Closing Prayer

Loving God,
you have given us responsibility
to continue your work on earth.
May we start with our families.
May we treat one another with
dignity and respect,
honour and kindness,
humility and truth,
gentleness and courage.
We make this prayer in the name of Jesus.
+**Amen.**

Extraordinary Women (Mother's Day)

She must be well attested for her good works, as one who has brought up children, shown hospitality, washed the saints' feet, helped the afflicted, and devoted herself to doing good in every way.
(1 Timothy 5:10)

Preparation: *Place flowers in a vase, a lit candle and an attractive basket containing paper cut-outs of flowers on the prayer table. As participants enter, give them a cut-out and a pencil. Ask them to write on it the name of their mother or of a person who has been like a mother to them. Have them place the cut-out in the basket. The prayer service will be dedicated to their mothers. Select readers.*

Invitation to Prayer

Mothers are extraordinary.
They take true delight in our baby steps
and share our anguish over our sorrows.
They bolster our spirits when we're down.

Mothers are unique.
They love us in spite of our faults,
encourage us in our distress,
and forgive us all our failings.

Mothers are irreplaceable.
They share the load of our burdens,
rejoice in our successes,
and support all our efforts.
Let us open our hearts to hear
the word of God.

+**Scripture**: Proverbs 31:25-31

Mother's Day Prayer

O loving God,
bless all mothers.
Bless their forgiving hearts,
their open arms,
their welcoming smiles.
Nurture their souls
All: As they nurture ours.
Care for their bodies
All: As they care for ours.
Pray for them
All: As they pray for us.
Teach them mercy and kindness
All: As they teach us.
Feed their hunger for knowledge
All: As they feed us.
Share your wondrous stories with them
All: As they share with us.
Love them always, despite their faults
All: As they love us.

O loving God,
bless all mothers.
Bless their forgiving hearts,
their open arms,
their welcoming smiles.
Bless all mothers.
Amen.

In honour of all mothers,
let us now pray to our Blessed and Holy
Mother Mary:
Hail Mary …

Closing Prayer

One person holds up the basket containing the paper cut-outs.

Loving God,
we dedicate this prayer service
to all those who mother us:
those of our present,
those of our past,
and those we have yet to meet.
Mothers who nurture us, care for us,
pray for us and teach us;
mothers who feed us, share with us
and love us.
We praise our Holy Mother Mary.
May we remain ever faithful
to those extraordinary women …
our mothers.
We ask this through your Son,
Jesus Christ our Lord.
+**Amen.**

Let Us Be Responsible

*Only live your life in a manner worthy of the gospel of Christ, so that, whether I come and see you or am absent and hear about you, I will know that you are standing firm in one spirit,
striving side by side with one mind
for the faith of the gospel.*
(Philippians 1:27)

Preparation: *Place a lit candle and a Bible on the prayer table. Select readers.*

Opening Prayer

✢God of trust,
help us to remain
accountable for the decisions we make,
loyal to the teachings of the Gospel,
dependable in all situations,
and constant in our honouring
of the tenets of our faith.
Help us to follow the model
of your Son Jesus.
Amen.

Scripture: Matthew 24:45-51

Litany: Let Us Be Responsible

Leader: There are many different facets of responsibility.
We ask God to guide us in our quest
to successfully access all these aspects.

Accountability

Let us be aware that others
will always be watching what we do.
They will question our actions.
**All: Let us be ready for their eyes
and ready to respond
when they ask us to explain our actions.
Let us be responsible.**

Dependability

Let us realize that others
will always be relying on us.
They will call on us in their time of need.
**All: Let us be able to answer their needs
and be prepared for their call.
Let us be responsible.**

Loyalty

Let us be conscious that others
will always attempt to sway us
to their opinion.
They will pull us to side with them instead.
**All: Let us be open to listen
to the thoughts of others,
but to always remain loyal
to the Gospel teachings.
Let us be responsible.**

Trustworthiness

Let us understand that others
will always expect us to keep their secrets.
They will trust us to honour their privacy.
**All: Let us ensure that we are faithful
to the hearts of others.
Let us not betray the confidence
of those around us.
Let us be responsible.**

Let us be accountable and loyal.
Let us be dependable and trustworthy.
**Let us be responsible.
Amen.**

Petitions

God of faith,
we pray to you with confidence,
love and open hearts.
The response to our petitions is:
God of faith, hear our prayer.

We are called to always follow the Word.
As we strive to be positive contributors
to the common good,
may we find wisdom and strength
in the teachings of the Gospels.
Let us pray to the Lord. **R.**

We are called to honour our commitments.
When we waver in our dedication
to promises made,
may God strengthen our resolve
and lead us along the right and true path.
Let us pray to the Lord. **R.**

We are called to remain true to ourselves.
When we struggle not to be swayed
by the opinion of the crowd,
may God gently remind us
to search our own hearts
for what we know to be just.
Let us pray to the Lord. **R.**
Amen.

Closing Prayer

Loving God,
we know that you depend on us
to be responsible citizens of the family
of Christ.
You expect us to be conscientious
and accountable for our actions,
open and honest in our prayers;
reliable and loving in our dealings with others.
Help us to remain steadfast and true
to your Gospel teachings.
Help us to be responsible.
We ask this through Jesus Christ our Lord.
+**Amen.**

The Season of Spring

[There is] a time to plant.
(Ecclesiastes 3:2)

Preparation: *Place a green tablecloth on your prayer centre. On it, place a large plate of green leaves. In the centre of the plate, light a green pillar candle. Divide the participants into two groups. Have representatives from Group 1 and Group 2 add tulips and sprigs from budding trees during the Litany. Select readers*

Opening Prayer

+God of the seasons,
you give us new life every spring.
We wake up and hear birds singing,
smell fragrant blossoms,
see tiny buds coming forth on the trees,
watch small animals scampering about,
and feel the warmth of the sun
and the gentle spring rains.
May we come to know you better
through this new life.
We ask this through your Son, Jesus Christ.
Amen.

Scripture: Song of Songs 2:11-13

Litany: Spring

Group 1: To the North, to the East,
to the South, to the West,
Leader: No matter where we look
during the season of spring,
God shows us the wonders of our world,
the glory of creation,
the splendours of life.

Group 2: Inward, outward
and all around us,
Leader: At every turn and within our heats,
we see new life emerging
as a sign of God's love for us all.
All: For God graces us children with the season of spring.

Leader: God blesses us with dewdrops
on a new morning,
Group 1: Delightfully fresh fragrances
and warm, gentle breezes,
Group 2: Chirping birds and
cherry blossoms,
Group 1: New saplings and
tiny emerging buds,
Group 2: Rushing water and
babbling brooks.
Group 1: From the North, from the East
Group 2: from the South, from the West,
Leader: No matter where we look,
and at every turn,
**All: God graces us children
with the season of spring.**
Amen.

Closing Prayer

God of new life,
during the season of spring,
we celebrate the Risen Lord, your Son Jesus,
and recognize the beauty of the earth,
your creation.
May we always offer you our prayers of
thanksgiving for the season of spring.
+**Amen.**

The Fire of the Holy Spirit (Pentecost)

The Holy Spirit fell upon them just as it had upon us at the beginning.
(Acts 11:15)

Preparation: *Drape the prayer table in red and place a lit red pillar candle on it. Add one glass pitcher that is full of water and three empty pitchers. (Glass is effective because it reflects the fire from the candle flame.) Divide participants into two groups for the Litany. Select readers.*

Opening Prayer

+O Holy Spirit,
light your cleansing fire within us.
Guide us to newness.
Lead us to living water.
Show us the way to freedom
by your power burning within us.
Amen.

Scripture: Acts 2:1-11, 16-18

Prayer of the Holy Spirit

During this prayer, pour some water from a full pitcher into three empty ones. Each time you pour, say, "Let the Holy Spirit be poured into us and set fire to our souls." Place the pitchers around the lit red candle to reflect the flame and represent the fiery presence of the Holy Spirit.

Leader: Let the Holy Spirit be poured into us and set fire to our souls.
O Holy Spirit!
Rest your tongue of fire upon us.

Group A: Set alight our souls.
Teach us to live according to your Word.

Group B: Show us how we may use your gifts to spread the Good News.

All: Let the Holy Spirit be poured into us and set fire to our souls.

Leader: O Holy Spirit!
Provide us with your life-giving water.

Group A: Pour into us wisdom,
that we may never thirst again.

Group B: Feed us with spiritual knowledge, that we may never hunger.

All: Let the Holy Spirit be poured into us and set fire to our souls.

Leader: O Holy Spirit!
Form a temple in our hearts.

Group A: Teach us to yearn for holiness.

Group B: Reveal to us the way to sacredness.

**All: Let the Holy Spirit be poured into us and set fire to our souls.
Amen.**

Reflection

"Veni Sancte" may be played or sung here as the reflection is read aloud.

Fire and water are biblical images of the Holy Spirit. In our lives, they represent strong forces in nature that can be both destructive and life giving. The Holy Spirit, too, causes flooding or burning away of evil and taint in our souls. This cleansing reveals a freshness and newness in which our gifts grow and flourish. Through the Holy Spirit, we gain access to God the Father. By the power of the Holy Spirit, the bread and wine at our eucharistic celebrations become the Body and Blood of our Saviour, Jesus. At this celebration of Pentecost, allow the Holy Spirit to touch your soul once more so you will be blessed by its life-giving power.

Closing Prayer

O Holy Spirit,
let your fire rest on each one of us.
Allow your power to give us new life
from within.
Lead us to the springs of life-giving water
so that we may cleanse our souls
and begin new life in you.
We ask this through Jesus Christ our Lord.
+**Amen.**

Hospitality and Hope
(The Feast of the Visitation, May 31)

Blessed is she who believed.
(Luke 1:45)

Preparation: *In the prayer centre, place a statue of Mary, a rosary, flowers, a Bible and a crucifix. Select readers.*

Opening Prayer

+Welcoming God,
you called Mary to give birth
to absolute Love.
You called Elizabeth to embrace Mary
with joy and reverence.
You call us to follow the example
of these courageous women
in our hoping and in our hospitality.
Amen.

Ritual: Sign of Welcome

Leader: Just as Elizabeth greeted Mary,
let us welcome with joy and reverence those
gathered here today.

All take a moment to greet each other.

Scripture: Luke 1:39-45

Scripture Reflection

Elizabeth, you welcomed your cousin
with warmth in your embrace and gladness
in your eyes. You welcomed one who was
gifted, yet troubled.
Gifted with the grace of giving birth
to the Messiah.
Troubled with the overwhelming
responsibility of the task
amid dark questions about parentage.

Remind us, Elizabeth,
to be open to the outsider,
to welcome the burdened soul,
to see each one of the children we serve
as bearers of God's grace.

God of meetings,
bless our greeting at gathering.
May we echo Elizabeth's joy and hospitality,
be carried by Mary's courage and hope,
and respond with our own Magnificats.

Magnificat (Luke 1:46-55)

Start with the leader alone. On the second line, the person to the right of the leader adds his or her voice. On the third line, the next person to the right joins in, and so on to the end of the Magnificat.

Leader: And Mary said, "My soul magnifies the Lord,
(line 2): and my spirit rejoices in God my Saviour,
(line 3): for he has looked with favour on the lowliness of his servant.
(line 4): Surely, from now on all generations will call me blessed;
(line 5): for the Mighty One has done great things for me,
(line 6): and holy is his name.
(line 7): Mercy is for those who respect God from generation to generation.
(line 8): God has shown strength.
(line 9): God has scattered the proud in the thoughts of their hearts.
(line 10): God has brought down the powerful from their thrones, and lifted up the lowly;

(line 11): God has filled the hungry with good things, and sent the rich away empty.
(line 12): God has helped his servant Israel, in remembrance of his mercy,
(line 13): according to the promise made to our ancestors, to Abraham
and to his descendants forever."

Blessing Prayer

Visit us, dear God,
in our homes and in our schools.
May we have eyes and hearts to see you
in stranger and friend alike.
May we be blessed by your companionship
and guidance,
now and always.
We make this prayer in the name of Jesus.
+**Amen.**

June

We Thank You (Retirement)

We were not idle when we were with you.
(2 Thessalonians 3:7)

Preparation: *Place a lit pillar candle on the prayer table to signify God's presence. Provide one taper for each retiree being celebrated. Select readers.*

Opening Prayer

+God of strength,
today we honour those individuals
who have shared their many talents
with their students, their colleagues
and their friends in education.
We thank you for the gift
of their presence among us.
They have shaped minds around them
by sowing seeds of independence,
instilling a thirst for knowledge,
sharing their friendship, and
exhibiting their love for you with their faith.
Faith is the ultimate education.
May they continue to be blessed by you
in all that they do, now and in the future.
We ask this through your Son,
Jesus Christ our Lord.
Amen.

Scripture: 2 Corinthians 9:6-15

Litany: Retirement

During the Litany, light the tapers from the candle on the prayer table and give a taper to each retiree.

Let us pray to God in thanksgiving
for all dedicated professionals
gathered here.

Over many years, you have given
your service, your time,
your gifts, your experience and your love
to your profession.

We thank you for your service.
You have shown us that
All: Performance speaks louder than words, commitment is the greatest offering, and wisdom exceeds material gain.

We thank you for your time.
You have shown us that
**All: Time is better spent getting to know the good in people
than getting to know their failings, and time is endless between friends.**

We thank you for your gifts.
You have shown us that
All: Everyone has something special to offer, and all gifts offered freely are valuable.

We thank you for experience.
You have shown us that there is
All: Knowledge beyond the classroom, intelligence beyond school lessons, and wisdom beyond textbooks.

Thank you for sharing your love.
You have shown us that
**All: You have something truly unique to share,
and that only through your love
could you share this with the world
and with those around you.
You have shared … you!**

We have been truly blessed.
All: We thank you for you.

Closing Prayer

God of life,
we honour those who have
generously given of their time and efforts
to their chosen professions.
They have followed your Word,
and we now reap the benefits of the riches
they have left behind them.
As they leave us,
may these friends know that,
though we will truly miss them,
their gifts live on in those
whose lives they have touched.
May you continue to bless them on their
ongoing faith journey to your kingdom.
Amen.

Closing Ritual

Leader: I invite you to bless each other with the sign of the cross.

Participants offer this blessing.

Harmonizing Word and Deed (Integrity)

Speak the truth to one another.
(Zechariah 8:16)

Preparation: *On the prayer focal point, place a cloth of the appropriate liturgical colour. Place on it a Bible, a candle and pictures of people who are symbols of integrity and honesty (such as the pope, saints, school patron). Select readers.*

Opening Prayer

+God of wisdom and truth,
you call us to be people of integrity,
to align our words with our deeds,
to remove hypocrisy from our agendas.
You ask us not only to speak truth
but to *be* truth.
Loving God, be with us on our journey
of discipleship.
Amen.

Scripture: Zechariah 8:16-17

Ritual

Leader: Let us take a few minutes of silence to reflect on the virtue of integrity using these guiding questions:

- When have I acted with integrity? (Think of two examples.)
- When did I fail to act with integrity? (Think of two examples.)
- What can I do to increase my integrity? (Name two actions.)

We bless our hearts, our heads and our hands with a sign of the cross to remind ourselves that we are called to be one in love, thought and deed.

Litany: Integrity

God of integrity,
lead us to unity in your love.
All: Make us one.
God of integrity,
help us to harmonize word and deed.
All: Make us one.
God of integrity,
lead us away from hypocrisy.
All: Make us one.
God of integrity,
give us courage to speak the truth.
All: Make us one.
God of integrity,
give us focus to see your light shining
through the darkness.
Amen.

Closing Prayer

Loving God,
you know our hearts
and you know our confusion.
Send your Spirit so we can understand
your Word in today's world.
Give us courage to echo your love honestly
and clearly to those around us.
May our deeds not contradict this message.
May this integrity be our hallmark
now and always.
We make this prayer in name of Jesus,
who is the way, the truth and the life.
+**Amen.**

Three in One (The Trinity)

The grace of the Lord Jesus Christ, the love of God, and the communion of the Holy Spirit be with all of you.
(2 Corinthians 13:13)

Preparation: *On the prayer table, place one large unlit pillar candle. Give three lit candles to three participants. When the service is about to begin and all are present, the three participants simultaneously light the larger candle with their candles. They may then place their candles in candle holders around the single larger candle. Select readers.*

Introduction

Leader: The central doctrine of our Catholic faith states that there is one God, and that God exists in three persons: God the Father, Creator of all things; God the Son, eternally begotten of the Father; and God the Spirit, who unites the Trinity. The three persons of God are co-eternal. From our first initiation into the Church with the sacrament of Baptism, we are blessed with holy oil using the Trinitarian formula: "In the name of the Father, and of the Son, and of the Holy Spirit." We continue our journey of faith in the love and joy of the Blessed Trinity, three in one.
Let us now listen to God's word.

Scripture: Matthew 28:16-20

Invitation to Prayer

When we pray, we begin with the sign of the cross. We bless ourselves in the name of the Trinity: in the name of the Father, and of the Son, and of the Holy Spirit.
Amen.

Litany: Blessed Be the Trinity

Three in one:
one in power, one in will, one in essence.
You are God in three persons.
Blessed be the Trinity.
**All: Three in one.
We believe in God in three persons:
Father, Son and Holy Spirit.
Blessed be the Trinity of our faith.**

God the Father,
you are the caring Creator of all things.
You understand all that we were,
all that we are, all that we hope to be.
You see all that we will become.
**All: Three in one.
We believe in God in three persons:
Father, Son and Holy Spirit.
Blessed be the Trinity of our faith.**

God the Son,
you are eternally begotten of the Father.
You are the God of humanity.
You understand what it is to be fully human:
to hunger, to thirst,
to tire, to feel pain, to love.
**All: Three in one.
we believe in God in three persons:
Father, Son and Holy Spirit.
Blessed be the Trinity of our faith.**

God the Holy Spirit,
you unite the Trinity.
It is through you that we
celebrate the sacraments.
It is through you that we have access
to God the Father and God the Son.

All: Three in one.
We believe in God in three persons:
Father, Son and Holy Spirit.
Blessed be the Trinity of our faith.

Three in one:
one in power, one in will, one in essence.
You are God in three persons.
Blessed be the Trinity.
All: Three in one.
We believe in God in three persons:
Father, Son and Holy Spirit.
Blessed be our God.
Blessed be the Trinity of our faith.
Amen.

Closing Reflection

The tallest and most stable human-made structures are on firm foundations with triangular bases: bases with three sides. Each single three-sided structure reaches up ever skyward. Our faith, too, is based on a firm foundation of three beings in one single God. We, too, reach ever upwards towards heaven. Three in one form the firm basis of our faith. Blessed be the Trinity.

Closing Ritual

All are invited to make the sign of the cross on their neighbour's forehead or hands.

On Being an Effective Communicator

*The Lord God has given me
the tongue of a teacher.*
(Isaiah 50:4)

Preparation: *On the prayer focal point, place a cloth in the appropriate liturgical colour. Place on it a Bible, a candle and various media, such as pen and paper, dictionary, DVD, cellphone, camera, artwork. Select readers.*

Opening Prayer

+God of all expression,
today we reflect on what it means
to be effective communicators.
Through our spoken and written words,
our art, and our acts of goodness,
may we honestly convey messages that
speak truly of your love for the world.
Amen.

Scripture: Mark 7:31-37

Scripture Reflection

Jesus cures the deaf and mute. He cures the blind. Not only are these profound miracles in themselves, but also they are symbols of Jesus' desire that the people be more effective communicators. The man wasn't cured so he could better hear stories about life's tragedies. His mouth wasn't opened so he could utter curses. The blind weren't given sight so they could focus on the ugliness of the world. Jesus healed the senses so that these people could love better. The symbolic dimension of these healings leads us to believe that Jesus also wants us to see the grace of God, sing with the heavenly choir, and hear the voice of love.

Ritual

Each person is invited to bless those beside them by tracing a sign of the cross over their eyes and ears while saying these words: "May you be blessed in word and deed."

Litany: Living in God's truth

God of the living Word,
you call us to be effective communicators.
All: Let us live in your truth.
God of the living Word,
you call us to speak, write and listen
honestly and sensitively.
Let us live in your truth.
All: Let us live in your truth.
God of the living Word,
you call us to respond critically
in light of Gospel values.
Let us live in your truth.
All: Let us live in your truth.

Closing Prayer

God of truth and integrity,
we praise you and thank you for the gifts
you have given your children.
May we know your truth and reflect it
in all we do and say.
May we be effective communicators
of your love and compassion.
May our schools be places where truth
is at home.
We make this prayer in the name of Jesus.
+**Amen.**

Called to Lead

*Obey my voice, and I will be your God,
and you shall be my people.*
(Jeremiah 7.23)

Preparation: *On the prayer focal point, place a cloth of the appropriate colour for the liturgical season. On the cloth place a candle, a Bible and a crucifix. Select readers.*

Call to Worship

+Lord of this world,
we work,
we watch,
we wait for you.

**All: Come down,
come in,
come among us.**

Lord of this life,
we labour,
we look,
we long for you.

**All: Come down,
come in,
come among us.**

Lord of this moment,
we strive,
we serve,
we search for you.

**All: Come down,
come in,
come among us,
That we may dwell in you
and you in us,
forever and ever.
Amen.**

Reflection

We are all leaders. Whether at work, at home, or in our friendship circles or clubs, we are all called to lead at some time. We all have our styles of leadership. Jesus pointed out that even those who are not the take-charge sorts are leaders by their example. The call to leadership can be disconcerting. Let us reflect on this call by looking at some of our heroes from Scripture..

Reader 1: God called from the burning bush, "Moses, I need you
to lead my people,
to liberate them,
to bring them to the promised land."

Reader 2: Moses replied,
"But God, I am slow of speech.
People laugh at my speech impediment.
Surely there is someone else?"

Reader 1: God said,
"Moses, I choose you to be a leader.
No matter what your disability,
my love is strong enough to work through you.
Go now and lead."

Reader 3: God said,
"Isaiah, I need you
to speak for me,
to remind my people
that they are my beloved."

Reader 4: Isaiah replied,
"But I am not good enough.
I speak bad words and bad ideas.
Surely there is someone else?"

Reader 3: God said,
"I will purify your heart;
I will give you the words
if you give me your ear.
Go now and lead."

Reader 5: God said,
"Jeremiah, I need you
to lead my people,
to remind them of the way to love
and justice in this time of darkness."

Reader 6: Jeremiah replied,
"But God, I am too young.
I am still a teen from the countryside.
The elders in the city will laugh at me.
Surely there is someone else?"

Reader 5: God said,
"Jeremiah, what you see as weakness,
I see as strength. You will have authority:
the authority that comes from
doing what is right and good.
When your words resonate with mine,
you shall be heard. Go now and lead."

Prayer

Dear God,
you have called us to lead.
There are times when we just don't feel up
to the task.
We look into the eyes of our colleagues
and think, "Why me? Do I deserve their
trust?"
Help us to know that we are doing
your will.
Give us the sense of peace
that is born of knowing that you are with us.
Give us the sense of faith
that is born of giving up our wills to you.
Give us the sense of love
that is born of forgiveness and communion.

May we always remember that
you are our leader –
you are our rod and our strength
on this journey.
We make this prayer through our leader,
our teacher, our companion, Jesus.
+**Amen.**

The Season of Summer

*As soon as [the branch of the fig tree] becomes tender
and puts forth its leaves,
you know that summer is near.*
(Matthew 24:32)

Preparation: *Place a pink tablecloth on your prayer centre. On it, place a large plate of green leaves. In the centre of the plate, place a lit pink pillar candle. Divide participants into two groups. Have representatives from each group add different types and colours of flowers (daisies, wildflowers, etc.) to the table during the Litany. Select readers.*

Opening Prayer

+God of the seasons,
you paint the world in a glorious array
of colour in summer.
We wake up to a pink sunrise and a green
world filled with blossoms of all kinds.
Gardens are flush with lovely flowers.
Trees are magnificent in their glory,
their branches growing ever upwards
towards the sun-filled sky.
Each summer you take our breath away
with the beauty you bestow upon us.
May we appreciate and be energized by
the spectacular colour
and majesty of your creation.
We ask this through Christ our Lord.
Amen.

Scripture: Joel 2:21-22

Litany: Summer

Group 1: To the north, to the east,
to the south, to the west,
Leader: No matter where we look
during the season of summer,
God shows us the wonders of our world,
the glory of creation,
the splendours of life.
Group 2: Inward, outward and all around us,
Leader: With every moment,
with every breath, with every glance,
we know that God is around us.
**All: For God graces us children
with the season of summer.**

Leader: God blesses us with the miracle
of sun-kissed land,
Group 1: Hot, still air and humid weather,
Group 2: Sunlit lakes, waterfalls and pools,
Group 1: Leafy trees and flower-filled
gardens,
Group 2: Long, lazy, hazy, sun-soaked
days.

Group 1: From the north, from the east,
from the south, from the west,
Leader: No matter where we look,
and at every turn,
**All: God graces us children
with the season of summer.**

Closing Prayer

God our Father,
during the season of summer,
extraordinary growth occurs in nature.
May we your children recognize
and celebrate the beauty of the earth
that you created,
and the time you give us to be renewed
and refreshed
and grow closer to you every year.
+**Amen.**

The Labyrinth of Life

For everyone who asks receives, and everyone who searches finds, and for everyone who knocks, the door will be opened.
(Matthew 7:8)

Preparation: *This prayer service is best done outdoors. Choose a quiet area where there is enough room to stand in a large circle and to wander randomly during the reflection period. If you must hold the service indoors, place chairs to form small, private nooks for quiet contemplation during the reflection. Begin the prayer service standing in a large circle facing inwards. Select readers.*

Opening Prayer

+God of life,
sometimes life is a maze of unknowns.
There are often unexpected twists and turns,
blocked passageways,
speed bumps and U-turns.
Sometimes the way seems plain,
and at other times it seems uncertain.
But whether the path is obvious or ambiguous,
smooth or pot-holed,
blocked or clear,
we know that you are always there
to see us through.
Help us to remember
that we need only ask you for directions
and for your guidance
as we move through the labyrinth of life.
We ask this through your Son,
our Guide, Jesus Christ.
Amen.

Scripture: Matthew 11:28-30 and Matthew 18:12-14

Litany: The Labyrinth of Life
When we meet up with unexpected roadblocks;
when we feel that we are not making progress;
when our life's journey feels as though it is still under construction;
when the road forks and we are unsure of what direction we should go;
**All: Walk with us, O God.
Guide us through the labyrinth of life.**

When the way is obscure
and the road is shrouded;
when we are uncertain of our final destination or the route we should take;
when life seems to be held in a precarious balance;
**All: Walk with us, O God.
Guide us through the labyrinth of life.**

When detours and twists in life overwhelm us;
when we feel there is nowhere to turn;
when we cannot even see the road;
when there appears to be no road map to follow;
when everything seems to be going wrong;
**All: Guide us, O God.
Guide us through the labyrinth of life.**

When the way seems clear enough;
when we are fairly certain
of which way to go
but seek advice to be absolutely sure;
when the road is unmistakable
but we are hesitant to traverse it alone;
**All: Walk with us, O God.
Guide us through the labyrinth of life.**

When the way is apparent
and the road is true;
when we are absolutely certain of our
destination and the route we should take;
when all in life seems to be
just as it should be;
**All: Walk with us, O God.
Guide us through the labyrinth of life.
For you are the way, the truth and the life.
You are the only road map we need.
You will see us safely through.
Walk with us, O God.
Guide us through the labyrinth of life.
Amen.**

Reflection

At this time, invite participants to freely wander and reflect on the following questions. After you have allowed a few minutes of quiet reflection, call them back to the circle for the Closing Prayer.

1. Can I see the road clearly? Do I ask for the Lord's help when I am lost?
2. Do I invite the Lord to walk with me in times of trial?
3. Do I remember to praise the Lord when the way is clear and easy, and all seems right in my life?
4. How can I help others who are travelling on the same road and are in difficulty?

Closing Prayer: The Labyrinth

Reader 1: Let the Lord God guide you.
**All: You can rest easy in God's hands,
for God will guide you through
the labyrinth of life.**

Reader 2: God knows the true path
and will stay with you always.
**All: You can rest easy in God's hands,
for God shows you the true path and will
stay with you through the labyrinth of life.**

Reader 3: God will always find you
and will surround you in love.
**All: You can rest easy in God's hands,
for God will find you
and will surround you with love
in this labyrinth of life.**

Reader 3: God will find you
and will surround you with love.
Reader 2: God shows you the true path
and will always stay with you.
Reader 1: God will guide you,
**All: For God is hope and truth and love,
and watches over us always
through the labyrinth of life.
+Amen.**

Journey into Summer

Well done, you good and faithful servant.
(Matthew 25:23, Good News Version)

Preparation: *In your prayer focal point, place on a green tablecloth a Bible, a candle and symbols of summer (such as a paperback novel, plastic beach pail and shovel, road map). Select readers.*

Opening Prayer

+Loving God,
you have walked with us
during this school year,
through the halls
and into the classrooms.
You have played with us in the gym
and schoolyard,
listened to us in our meetings,
touched us when we grieved,
celebrated with us in our joy.
We thank you for your presence
and guidance.
As we look forward to the slower pace
that summer brings,
may we grow in the knowledge
that you are always in our midst.
Amen.

Scripture: Philippians 1:3-11

Reflection

We are called to be a community
of gratitude and hope.
We are so grateful for our colleagues.
They are icons of your love,
companions in service
and a blessing to the school.

Ritual

Leader: I would like to call those who will not be at the school with us next year to come forward. The rest of the community is invited to come up and give each person a blessing (sign of the cross on the forehead or hands, or a hand on the shoulder) and some personal words of farewell.

Litany: Before We Go

God of love,
throughout this year, you have gathered us
to create community,
to hear the Good News with new ears, and
to bring a message of hope to the world.

Driven by a commitment to justice,
drawn by the beauty of life,
we look at our world:
its blessedness and its fragility.

God of compassion,
All: Before you we place our broken world, marred by violence and neglect.
God of mercy,
All: Before you we place our broken communities, marred by isolation and despair.
God of healing,
All: Before you we place our broken hearts, marred by fear and loneliness.
God of joy,
All: Before you we place our dreams and visions: bless them.
God of hope,
All: Before you we place our labour of love: bless our work.
God of goodness,
All: Before you we place our gratitude for life: bless us and our community.

Closing Prayer

God of wonder and love,
during this school year you summoned us
to work with you
to help build a Civilization of Love.
May we reflect on the lessons
of our time together
so we can make next year even better
than this year.
May we reflect your wisdom and love
to those we serve and work with.
May we grow to understand
that we sow seeds
that will not be harvested for some time.

God of mercy and forgiveness,
help us to understand that
our incompleteness is a gift:
a way to reach out to the other,
a way of inviting the other to minister to us.
Be with us always.

May we open our hearts to
wisdom and song,
joy and wonder,
truth and compassion,
peace and tranquility,
this day and always.
+**Amen.**

Index

Saints and Witnesses

A Cloud of Witnesses	28
Lead Us in the Footsteps of the Saints (All Saints' Day)	37
Choose Peace (Remembrance Day)	40
Mary Said "Yes"	54
The True Nature of God (St. Thomas Aquinas)	71
Daughters of Faith (International Women's Day)	93
God of the Journey (St. Patrick's Day)	97
You Called Mary (Annunciation)	98
Servants of Love (Administrative Professionals' Day)	113
Model of Love (St. Joseph the Worker)	115
Hospitality and Hope (The Feast of the Visitation, May 31)	126
We Thank You (Retirement)	129

The Liturgical Year

Advent I: Hope	56
Advent II: Faith	57
Advent III: Joy	58
Advent IV: Love	59
Preparing for Christmas	60
New Beginnings (New Year)	62
To Be Your People (Epiphany)	64
The True Nature of God (St. Thomas Aquinas)	71
Lead Us into the Desert (Ash Wednesday)	82
Desert, Teach Me (Prayers for Reconciliation)	84
Lent I: Renewal	85
Lent II: Sacrifice	88
Lent III: Resisting Temptation	90
Lent IV: To Serve Others	92
God of the Journey (St. Patrick's Day)	97
You Called Mary (Annunciation)	98
Into Jerusalem (Beginning of Holy Week)	100
Help Us to Love (Stations of the Cross)	102
The Upper Room (Holy Thursday)	105
Easter Light	106
Easter Blessing	108
Model of Love (St. Joseph the Worker)	115
The Fire of the Holy Spirit (Pentecost)	124
Hospitality and Hope (The Feast of the Visitation, May 31)	126
Three in One (The Trinity)	132
Lead Us in the Footsteps of the Saints (All Saints' Day)	37
Comfort Us Today (All Souls' Day)	39
Mary Said "Yes"	54

Prayer Services for the Academic Year

Our Dreams and Our Cares: Welcoming New Teachers	13
To Be Instruments of Your Healing: A New School Year	14
Jesus the Teacher	16
The Work of Our Hands	20
Encircle Our School (Curriculum Night)	21
Open the Eyes of Our Hearts (Professional Activity Day)	23
The Blessed Vocation of Teaching	25
Choose Peace (Remembrance Day)	40
Building Bridges Between Parents and Teachers	53
New Beginnings (New Year)	62
Sowing the Seeds of Your Love (New Semester)	76
March Break Blessing	96
God of the Journey (St. Patrick's Day)	97
You Called Mary (Annunciation)	98
Speak to the Earth (Earth Week)	111
Servants of Love (Administrative Professionals' Day)	113
Created in Your Image (Catholic Education Week)	116
We Thank You (Retirement)	129
Called to Lead	135
Journey into Summer	140

Prayer Services about God, Jesus and the Holy Spirit

Jesus the Teacher	16
God Gives Us Courage	18
God Has Compassion	30
Discerning Believer	31
God's Gift of Life	34
Living Water	46
What Would Jesus Do? (Social Justice)	48
Respect the Word of the Lord	50
Preparing for Christmas	60
In God's Time	66
We are United in Christ	68
We Believe	73
God's Love for Us	80
God Will Be There	81
God of the Journey (St. Patrick's Day)	97
You Called Mary (Annunciation)	98
Into Jerusalem (Beginning Holy Week)	100
Help Us to Love (Stations of the Cross)	102
The Upper Room (Holy Thursday)	105
Easter Light	106
Easter Blessing	108
Our Greatest Gift (Reverence)	110

Created in Your Image (Catholic Education Week) 116
The Fire of the Holy Spirit (Pentecost) 124
Three in One (The Trinity) 132

Virtues and Catholic Graduate Expectations

God Gives Us Courage 18
On Being a Lifelong Learner 19
Gratitude 29
God Has Compassion 30
Discerning Believer 31
A Vision of Justice 42
Building a Civilization of Love (Being a Responsible Citizen) 44
What Would Jesus Do? (Social Justice) 48
Respect the Word of the Lord 50
Being a Collaborative Contributor (Collaboration) 69
Let Us Praise Wisdom 78
Desert, Teach Me (Prayers for Reconciliation) 84
Lent III: Resisting Temptation 90
Answer the Call to Persevere 95
Our Greatest Gift (Reverence) 110
On Being a Caring Family Member 117
Let Us Be Responsible 121
Harmonizing Word and Deed (Integrity) 131
On Being an Effective Communicator 134
Called to Lead 135

Secular and Seasonal Celebrations

The Season of Autumn 27
Gratitude 29
Choose Peace (Remembrance Day) 40
Healing and Hope (World AIDS Day) 52
New Beginnings (New Year) 62
The Season of Winter 65
Let Us Celebrate Our Differences 77
Daughters of Faith (International Women's Day) 93
March Break Blessing 96
Speak to the Earth (Earth Week) 111
Servants of Love (Administrative Professionals' Day) 113
Extraordinary Women (Mother's Day) 119
The Season of Spring 123
We Thank You (Retirement) 129
The Season of Summer 137
Journey into Summer 140